The Rhetoric of Redemption

Communication, Media, and Politics
Series Editor: Robert E. Denton, Jr., Virginia Tech

This series features a broad range of work dealing with the role and function of communication in the realm of politics, broadly defined. Including general academic books, monographs, and texts for use in graduate and advanced undergraduate courses, the series will encompass humanistic, critical, historical, and empirical studies in political communication in the United States. Primary subject areas include campaigns and elections, media, and political institutions. *Communication, Media, and Politics* books will be of interest to students, teachers, and scholars of political communication from the disciplines of communication, rhetorical studies, political science, journalism, and political sociology.

Titles in the Series

The Millennium Election: Communication in the 2000 Campaign
Edited by Lynda Lee Kaid, John C. Tedesco, Dianne G. Bystrom, and Mitchell McKinney
Strategic Political Communication: Rethinking Social Influence, Persuasion, and Propaganda
Karen S. Johnson-Cartee and Gary A. Copeland
Campaign 2000: A Functional Analysis of Presidential Campaign Discourse
William L. Benoit, John P. McHale, Glenn J. Hansen, P. M. Pier, and John P. McGuire
Inventing a Voice: The Rhetoric of American First Ladies of the Twentieth Century
Edited by Molly Meijer Wertheimer
Communicating for Change: Strategies of Social and Political Advocates
John P. McHale
Political Campaign Communication: Principles and Practices, Fifth Edition
Judith S. Trent and Robert V. Friedenberg
The Rhetoric of Redemption: Burke's Redemption Drama and King's "I Have a Dream" Speech
David A. Bobbitt

Forthcoming

Reelpolitik II: Political Ideologies in '50s and '60s Films
Beverly Merrill Kelley
New Frontiers in International Communication Theory
Edited by Mehdi Semati
Entertaining Politics: New Political Television and Civic Culture
Jeffrey P. Jones
Women's Political Discourse
Molly A. Mayhead and Brenda DeVore Marshall
The 2004 Presidential Campaign: A Communication Perspective
Edited by Robert E. Denton, Jr.
Politeness and Political Debate
Edward A. Hinck, Shelly S. Hinck, and William O. Dailey
Media and the Staging of American Politics
Gary C. Woodward

The Rhetoric of Redemption

Kenneth Burke's Redemption Drama and Martin Luther King, Jr.'s "I Have a Dream" Speech

David A. Bobbitt

ROWMAN & LITTLEFIELD PUBLISHERS, INC.
Lanham • Boulder • New York • Toronto • Oxford

ROWMAN & LITTLEFIELD PUBLISHERS, INC.

Published in the United States of America
by Rowman & Littlefield Publishers, Inc.
A wholly owned subsidiary of The Rowman & Littlefield Publishing Group, Inc.
4501 Forbes Boulevard, Suite 200, Lanham, MD 20706
www.rowmanlittlefield.com

P.O. Box 317, Oxford OX2 9RU, UK

British Library Cataloguing in Publication Information Available

Library of Congress Cataloging-in-Publication Data Available

ISBN: 978-0-7425-2928-1

Printed in the United States of America

∞™ The paper used in this publication meets the minimum requirements of American National Standard for Information Sciences—Permanence of Paper for Printed Library Materials, ANSI/NISO Z39.48-1992.

This book is dedicated to the memory of my mother and father, Mary Bobbitt (1929–1995) and Charles Bobbitt (1928–1970).

Contents

Preface

More than forty years after its presentation, Martin Luther King's "I Have a Dream" speech still resonates with the American consciousness. It is one of the most famous and critically acclaimed speeches in American history. King's vivid images of racial harmony still serve as a vision, in the minds of many people, of what America can and should be. What gives this speech its power? How come excerpts from the speech are still played on television and in classrooms across America to the point that most adults, and many children born two or three decades after the speech was delivered, can recite parts of the speech word for word?

In this book I will attempt to answer those questions. In doing so I will rely heavily upon the work of Kenneth Burke, perhaps the most influential American rhetorical theorist of the twentieth century. This book presents a development of Kenneth Burke's theory of guilt-purification-redemption, and applies that theory to Martin Luther King, Jr.'s "I Have a Dream" speech. Because of the focus by rhetorical scholars on Burke's pentad, his redemption drama has been an often overlooked aspect of his theory. Such studies as we do have of the cycle of guilt-purification-redemption have emphasized victimage and mortification as modes of purification. Here I develop aspects of the victimage/mortification family of purificatory modes not previously noted by Burke or Burkean scholars and identify and develop other Burkean modes of purification—purification through transcendence and purification through images of change, movement, and dramatic catharsis.

I argue that King's "I Have a Dream" speech may be studied as the "representative anecdote" of the first phase of the civil rights movement. I maintain that the "I Have a Dream" speech derives its rhetorical appeal from its enactment of the Burkean redemption drama in which preexistent guilt is symbolically purified through (a) victimage and mortification, (b) transcendence, and (c) images of change, movement, and dramatic catharsis. King's metaphors are also analyzed in order to demonstrate how they contribute to the overall drama enacted in the speech.

As one of the most well-known speeches of modern times, and as a representative, authorizing text on race relations in America, it is crucial that communication scholars, political scientists, historians, and scholars of African American studies understand the symbolic inducements from which this speech derives its appeal. Because of the near-mythic status this speech has taken on in the popular mind, it has influenced subsequent thought and discourse on race relations in America. Thus, an understanding of the speech as a redemption drama allows us to see thought patterns that developed from the rhetorical appeals represented by this address.

My purpose will be to answer the following questions:

1. What is the message/form of this speech?[1] In other words, to what underlying symbolic inducements are auditors responding? What are its myths? What authority, hierarchy, and order does it invoke and evoke? What conflicts and contradictions does it attempt to transcend and how?
2. Why did this particular message/form emerge from the competing voices on civil rights to capture the public imagination? What competing voices did the speech mute or ignore?
3. What are the shortcomings of this message/form? What are its limitations and contradictions? What thought patterns does it encourage and discourage? What learned dysfunctions does it produce?
4. What is the legacy of the speech? In other words, to what degree did the success of the speech's message/form contribute to the civil rights movement's eventual failure to achieve its goals beyond the dismantling of legal segregation?
5. Finally, what will the answers to the above questions reveal about the short-term and long-term effects of a successful, totalizing rhetoric of assimilation? Does the need to transcend differences in such a discourse always result in an elision of the practical difficulties of achieving assimilation? Are there other means available to a rhetor under such circumstances; that is, can real, bitter, long-term divisions of race, class, religion, and so on, be transcended by being integrated under a higher good without ignoring the sociopolitical difficulties of effecting such assimilation?

The answers to these question are significant in two respects: the first methodological, the second historical-critical. First, while Burke's guilt-purification-redemption model has been partially developed and aspects of it have been applied, the model has not been fully developed and applied. Most studies concentrate on victimage and/or mortification as modes of purification. This book will examine other modes of purification indicated by Burke, but not developed by Burke or Burkean scholars. Purification through images of change and movement and the purificatory effect of dramatic catharsis in rhetorical discourse have not been examined by rhetorical scholars. In addition, the very common and significant rhetorical technique of transcendence has not received as much study as it deserves, nor has its use as a means of absolving guilt been fully explored.

Second, this book provides the first complete scholarly analysis of the most influential speech of the civil rights movement and arguably the most significant American political speech of the twentieth century (American Rhetoric, Top 100 Speeches, 2002). King's "I Have a Dream" speech has been widely praised, but not thoroughly examined. This study reveals the sources of its effectiveness and assesses King's rhetorical choices. Understanding the sources of this speech's effectiveness will increase our understanding of the rhetorical success of the first phase of the civil rights movement and aid in a comprehension of the speech's lasting impact on American culture. It will allow a critical evaluation of the ideas that proved so persuasive in ending legal segregation and securing long-denied basic civil rights for African Americans, while providing an assessment of the long-term implications of those rhetorical choices.

Wenzel (1989) argues that rhetorical critics should not "stand in awe of a speech just because it occupies a prominent place on the canvas of history. Rather, we should endeavor to understand it and evaluate it on its own terms, as a real response to a particular situation" (p. 179). This study seeks to analyze the speech as a real response to a particular historical-political situation, but also endeavors to understand why the speech has become iconized by being extracted from its historical-political context and turned into a mythic, and almost sacred, text.

Chapter 1 places "I Have a Dream" within the context of the civil rights movement as a whole, and shows how the speech can be seen as the paradigmatic discourse of the movement. Previous scholarship on the speech is considered and the critical approaches used in this book will be explained.

Chapter 2 describes the intellectual influences upon the agent, Martin Luther King, which are manifested in the act, the "I Have a Dream" speech. The section on agent also demonstrates how the ideas employed in the "Dream" speech were recurring themes employed by King since the beginning of his public career. The discussion of the scene examines the context in which the speech took place by describing the historical scene, the intermediate scene, and the immediate scene.

Chapter 3 commences the analysis of the speech itself as a redemption drama in which the audience's preexistent guilt is symbolically purified. After discussion of the audiences addressed by, and the reaction to, the speech, the chapter describes how King's symbolic response to the scene takes the form (representative anecdote) of Burke's guilt-purification-redemption drama. The statistical and cluster analysis, and pentadic ratio analysis of the speech, are also here presented. Finally, the guilt phase of the redemption drama is described through a discussion of Burke's theory of guilt and a demonstration of how preexistent guilt is symbolically manifested in King's address.

Chapter 4 discusses the methods by which King's speech symbolically purifies the audience of their guilt. It describes purification through victimage and mortification, purification through transcendence, and purification through images of change, movement, and dramatic catharsis. Finally, the temporary state of redemption to which King has brought his audience is discussed.

Chapter 5 analyzes King's metaphors to determine how his choice of metaphors helps constitute the message/form of the speech. After a brief history of the theory of metaphor demonstrating the role of metaphor in meaning-creation, three metaphoric clusters are examined: the "check/promissory note" cluster, the dark/light cluster, and the "dream" cluster.

Chapter 6 evaluates the theory of guilt-purification-redemption and what this book has revealed about the usefulness of it as a critical methodology. Here I analyze Burke's theory of guilt, consider what new information this book has provided about the Burkean modes of purification, and examine how the guilt-purification-redemption model functions as a cultural form of experience.

Chapter 7 considers the significance and legacy of the "I Have a Dream" speech. Chapter 8 summarizes the findings of this book.

While any errors, omissions, and faults are entirely my own, I do owe a great deal of gratitude to a number of people who gave of their time and knowledge to help me with this book. I want to thank Andrew King for reading this manuscript numerous times and for his ideas, insights, and support. I carried this book and gave birth to it, but Andy was the midwife. I am very grateful to Robert Denton for his guidance and encouragement. He expertly stewarded this book through the editorial process. I would also like to thank Harold Mixon and Kenneth Zagacki. Their suggestions upon reading earlier versions of the manuscript have greatly improved the final product. I want to thank Nanette Jaynes for reading an earlier draft and providing me with valuable advice. I also wish to express my appreciation to Brenda Hadenfeldt, Erica Fast, and Kärstin Painter at Rowman & Littlefield for guiding this book through the production process and answering my many questions.

The research for this book was conducted using the resources of several libraries and archives that deserve my gratitude. I would like to thank the staffs at the Troy H. Middleton Library at Louisiana State University in Baton Rouge, the King Library and Archives at the Martin Luther King, Jr. Center for Nonviolent Social Change in Atlanta, the Mississippi Valley Collection at the University of Memphis Library, and the Lucy Lester Willet Memorial Library at Wesleyan College in Macon, Georgia.

NOTE

1. While form and content can be abstracted from one another for purposes of study, any thorough consideration of content necessarily entails a consideration of form. See Burke (1969b, p. 65) and Duncan (1962, p. 320).

1

Context and Critical Methodologies

The movement for civil rights for African Americans that took place during the 1950s and 1960s was one of the most successful social movements in American history. It was "a rare and stunning achievement of liberation" (Graham, 1990, p. 452) that forever altered the social and political landscape of America. Within a dozen years it toppled a system of legal segregation and discrimination against African Americans that had been in place more than half a century. The civil rights movement was probably the most significant domestic development in post–World War II America. Its tactics provided the model, and its success provided the inspiration, for the many subsequent social reform movements of the 1960s and 1970s—the student movement, the antiwar movement, the women's movement, the gay rights movement, and others (Chafe, 1986, pp. 127–128; Rorabaugh, 2002, p. 57).

While the civil rights movement became the paradigm for subsequent social movements, Martin Luther King's "I Have a Dream" speech became the paradigmatic discourse of the civil rights movement. Garrow (1986a) called it "the rhetorical achievement of a lifetime, the clarion call that conveyed the moral power of the movement's cause to the millions who had watched the live national network coverage" (p. 284). Gentile (1983) believes the speech "forever 'legitimized' the civil rights movement to those whites who had difficulty accepting it" (p. 249). The speech has been widely anthologized and repeatedly excerpted on television to the extent that it is probably the most well-known speech in American history. Many, if not most, Americans can recite at least a few lines from King's famous "dream" sequence which climaxes the speech. Leff (1987) calls the speech "an emblem of our culture" which has "become part of our lived experience." Payne (1989) says the "I Have a Dream" speech is a "historical and cultural artifact" (p. 47) and Dyson

(2000) says it is "one of the defining moments of American civic rhetoric" (p. 16). The speech has become so much a part of the nation's shared experience of public discourse that the phrase "the Dream" is often used as a shorthand expression for a vision of an America of racial harmony and justice. The speech has become woven into the fabric of American history and public culture, partaking of and adding to the great American myth of renewal and rebirth, of a nation where people can transcend their past and start over. King's speech gave America a vision of itself overcoming its past of slavery, segregation, and racial crimes, bringing African Americans into the "melting pot" of American community.

This book examines "I Have a Dream" as the "representative anecdote" (Burke, 1969a, pp. 59–61) of the first phase of the civil rights movement. The modern-day civil rights movement in America involved two general phases. Phase one included the campaigns for the elimination of overt segregation and the demand for the recognition of basic legal rights for African Americans. This phase culminated in the two main legislative achievements of the civil rights era, the Civil Rights Act of 1964 and the Voting Rights Act of 1965. After 1965, phase two of the movement shifted from an emphasis on nondiscrimination and equal treatment before the law, to a concern with equal results in the distribution of economic resources through affirmative action programs for minorities (Graham, 1990, pp. 456–457; Thorton, 1986, pp. 148–151).

The 1965–66 period marked a watershed for the civil rights movement in another respect as well. While the modern-day civil rights movement had been riddled with organizational and personal rivalries almost from its inception in the mid-1950s, these had largely been contained and ameliorated through the need to work together for a common goal. For the 1963 March on Washington, all five major civil rights organizations—the National Association for the Advancement of Colored People (NAACP), the National Urban League (NUL), the Congress of Racial Equality (CORE), the Southern Christian Leadership Conference (SCLC), and the Student Nonviolent Coordinating Committee (SNCC)—managed to pull together and cooperate despite underlying tensions. After 1965, however, the disagreements within the movement became more intense and more public. SNCC and CORE became more radical as "black power" advocates assumed leadership of these organizations. By mid-1966 the movement was publicly splitting apart over the "black power" controversy, the advocacy of violence by some of its more extreme elements, and the issue of whether the movement should be linked to opposition to the Vietnam War (Weiss, 1986, p. 54). The movement no longer even agreed on fundamental objectives. For the more radical elements of the movement the objective of integration gave way to the goal of black separatism, and a more collectivist vision replaced the ideal of individual liberty and opportunity. While never advocating violence or abandoning the goal of integration, even Martin Luther King sharpened his critique of American society and moved in the direction of economic collectivism in the last few years of his public career (Chafe, 1986, pp. 134–136; Dyson, 2000, pp. 78–90; Lischer, 1995, pp. 160–162; Thorton, 1986, p. 150).

Seeing the civil rights movement as taking place in two phases allows us to contextualize the "Dream" speech in its proper historical and cultural milieu. While it did not articulate the metanarrative of the movement in its second phase, the "Dream" speech did define the metaphysical form of the movement in its first phase. Yet "I Have a Dream" has been passed down to subsequent generations as the authenticating discourse of "the civil rights movement." This is because phase one of the movement was equalitarian in its ideology and assimilationist in its objectives. Its emphasis on individual rights was consistent with traditional American values. Yet equality was not achieved in phase one of the civil rights movement because of the difficulty of overcoming historical divisions not easily mitigated. Phase two was shaped by the frustration resulting from the failure of the assimilationist model to provide immediate results, so it revived a model which emphasized black self-empowerment, black identity, and black separatism. It is phase one of the civil rights movement—when the fight was against legally sanctioned segregation and the goal was integration and equal opportunity—that most people mean today when they speak of "the civil rights movement." This was the era of the historic battles and the great moral victories—the Montgomery bus boycott, the student sit-ins, the Freedom Rides, the Birmingham campaign, the Selma campaign—that have become enshrined in the annals of the movement. This was the era of George Wallace, "Bull" Connor, and Jim Clark, who became forever etched in the nation's consciousness as personifications of the arch-segregationist. And this was the era of the now legendary March on Washington, the largest demonstration for human rights in the nation's history up to that time, where the movement proved that it could gather over a quarter of a million people, black and white, together in a spirit of peace and brotherhood without violence, and where King delivered his famous speech.

"I Have a Dream" captured the public imagination so completely that it constructed the symbolic syntax from which the nation has drawn its subsequent discourse about civil rights. The speech became the dominant discursive act that gave the movement its form by articulating its focus, purpose, strategy, myths, and language. But as a result of its success the speech's message has come to be treated as axiomatic or creedal, instead of as a text still open to analysis and criticism. Its images are appealed to, its logic is seen as authorizing, and its narrative is viewed as the only proper path for race relations in America. In short, it has become a powerful piece of American mythology in its own right. This has resulted in some reluctance on the part of rhetorical scholars to criticize the speech as they would any other speech, to analyze it for its shortcomings as a model for race relations, and to point out how its reliance on secular myth and religious imagery causes King's vision to depend on a traditional conception of national identity and purpose that has become increasingly inadequate, since the social and cultural changes of the 1960s, to sustain communal cohesion and guide social reform. Thus, most studies of this speech seek mainly to praise its greatness and ascertain the techniques of its rhetorical appeal (one exception is Hariman, 1989).

PREVIOUS STUDIES OF THE "I HAVE A DREAM" SPEECH

Considering its significance, it is surprising that so few scholars have attempted a thorough analysis of the "I Have a Dream" speech. Alvarez (1988) argued that the speech adopts the characteristics of the black Baptist sermon, with its dialogue form, use of common knowledge (from the Bible, a black spiritual, and secular texts), and its use of figures of speech such as antithesis, extended metaphors, periphrasis, and anaphora. Miller's (1989) work also emphasized the effect of the black folk pulpit on King's ideas and persuasiveness in this speech. He argued that the black folk pulpit traditions of voice merging and self-making (incorporating common knowledge from the Bible or other sources into one's text, thus assuming the persona of the source), and typological epistemology (drawing parallels between biblical events and current events) enabled King to "reanimate stereotyped expressions" (p. 26). Cox (1989) examined the speech as a reconstitution of the concept of "public time" for social change in response to the "gradualism" advocated by white moderates. In a response to Cox, Hariman (1989) argued that King's sense of urgency came primarily from the leadership struggle that was occurring within the civil rights movement (p. 207). He maintained that while King may have established that the time had come for legislative action, the speech "also suggested that civil disobedience and the radical demand for social transformation had become untimely, out of synch with the American Dream" (p. 216). Patton (1993) finds the speech reflects essential features of orality by employing a form of preaching known as kerygma in which the preacher is seen as presenting the revealed word of God. Solomon (1993) argues the speech derives its power from an implied matrix metaphor that underlies its structure and generates its rich imagery.

No study of King's "Dream" speech has employed Burke's theory of guilt-purification-redemption, which this analysis uses. In addition, no scholarly study of this speech has gone beyond an article-length analysis of King's inventional choices or identification of the rhetorical patterns and appeals the speech employs. While my analysis does not attempt to refute the thesis of any of the above-mentioned studies of the "Dream" speech—in fact, all, to one degree or another, reinforce my arguments—it does go beyond these studies to identify the basic structure of the speech as a guilt-purification-redemption drama, and to examine the implications of King's use of this rhetorical form.

Shortly before this book went to press I came across Hansen's (2003) book on the "I Have a Dream" speech. While Hansen is not a communication theorist or critic and his book does not present a scholarly analysis of the speech, he does provide a valuable description of the compositional process the "Dream" speech went through. He also argues that the speech did not achieve its full significance as a defining text of American public culture until the late 1970s and early 1980s.

DRAMATISM

In this book I use the theories of Kenneth Burke. Specifically, I develop and employ his theory of guilt-purification-redemption (sometimes referred to as the "redemption drama"). However, Burke's redemption drama is part of his larger dramatistic system, which I will also be drawing upon. Burke (1969a) termed his overall methodology dramatism because "it invites one to consider the matter of motives in a perspective that, being developed from an analysis of drama, treats language and thought primarily as modes of action" (p. xxii). Motive is a key concept in Burke's theory. Human action does not have absolute meaning in and of itself. We explain our actions in terms of motives. To explain one's conduct in terms of a particular motive is to adopt the orientation accepted by one's social group. Since motives are shorthand explanations for situations, an analysis of motives is an analysis of human behavior. Since motives are also linguistically constructed, an analysis of motives requires an analysis of language (Burke, 1984b, pp. 19–36). Burke (1968b) defines dramatism as "a method of analysis and corresponding critique of terminology designed to show the most direct route to the study of human relations and human motives is via a methodical inquiry into cycles or clusters of terms and their functions" (p. 445).

Burke's (1966) critical system revolves around his definition of the human being as "the symbol-using animal" (pp. 3–9) and his notion that to use language is to engage in "symbolic action" (p. 63). Human beings are distinctively symbol-using creatures whose actions and interactions are carried out through the exchange of symbols. When human beings use symbols, they are involved in "action." Act is thus the key term of dramatism from which related concepts derive. For there to be an act, there must be an agent. Similarly, there must be a scene in which the agent acts, through some means or agency, involving some purpose (Burke, 1968b, pp. 445–446; 1969a, p. xv). Act, agent, agency, scene, and purpose are the five key terms of the dramatistic pentad, corresponding to the journalistic questions what, who, how, where, and why.

Dramatism is particularly suited to a study of King's rhetoric. As Burke has noted, the concept of dramatism is drawn from literature. Literary drama involves conflict, or agon, between good and bad. The conflict is resolved in some manner that leaves the situation changed from the status quo ante, but in the process certain principles of good and bad are upheld, amended, or destroyed. King, like Gandhi whose tactics he adopted, realized that nonviolent social protest is basically an art form which requires the staging of dramatic moral confrontations with the enemy (Colaiaco, 1988, p. 2), the purpose of which is to win sympathy to one's cause while revealing the immorality of the opponent's position (see Garrow, 1978, pp. 220–231; M. L. King, 1958, pp. 216–217; 1986, pp. 7–8). In other words, King orchestrated "sociodramas," staged struggles "between good and bad principles of social order" (Duncan, 1968, p. 34). In social dramas actors struggle to uphold, destroy, or change principles of social order by seeking "to control symbols that are already powerful, or to create new symbols that will make orderly relationships that cannot be made orderly through the use of traditional or sacred symbols" (Duncan, 1968, p. 64). As Griffin (1969) has noted, "To study a movement is to study a drama, an Act of transformation, an Act that ends in transcendence, the achievement of salvation" (p. 462).

Although Burke has never provided a synthetic explanation of all of the elements in the methodology of dramatism, Conrad (1984) maintained that dramatistic criticism involves three steps: first, a statistical analysis of terms involving an inductive search for the dramatic alignment of the work; second, the search for the representative anecdote; and third, pentadic analysis. The first and third steps will be developed further in the course of this study (see chapter 3), but since I am arguing for the treatment of King's "I Have a Dream" as a representative anecdote, I will consider this concept now.

REPRESENTATIVE ANECDOTE

Burke (1969a) wrote that dramatism "involves the search for a 'representative anecdote' to be used as a form in conformity with which the vocabulary is constructed" (p. 59). Crable (2000) argues that the representative anecdote is central to Burke's theory of dramatism. There is some debate among Burkean scholars as to whether a representative anecdote is a particular discursive act representative of a larger body of discourse or an underlying narrative form embedded within the discourse. However, Madsen (1993) maintains that the representative anecdote can be both act and form (pp. 208–211). If a particular discursive act can be shown to be representative of a larger body of discourse, then the underlying narrative form or synecdochal narrative embedded in that act is tautologically representative of the larger body of discourse. Thus, this study treats King's "I Have a Dream" as representative of a larger body of civil rights discourse (that of the moderate wing of the first phase of the civil rights movement) and seeks the underlying representative anecdote (synecdochal narrative) which constructs the speech.

Drawing from Burke's own writings and other studies of Burke's concept of representative anecdote, Madsen (1993) posits three criteria for determining if an anecdote is representative: (1) human action and symbol use, (2) scope, and (3) synecdoche (pp. 212–214). The first criterion is that the representative anecdote must reflect human action and choice instead of sheer motion or physical relationships (Conrad, 1984, p. 98). Since humans respond to symbols, a truly representative case of human motivation must be linguistic. This criterion eliminates nonsymbolic, deterministic, and mechanistic representations of human action such as conditioned reflex or a railway terminal, which Burke (1969a) rejects as representative anecdotes for human motives and communication respectively (pp. 59, 326–327). Secondly, the representative anecdote must possess scope, that is, it "must be supple and complex enough to be representative of the subject matter it is designed to calculate" (Burke, 1969a, p. 60). If an anecdote is to be truly representative of a larger constellation of discourse, it must faithfully reflect that discourse by incorporating "many or most of the terms or particulars of [that] discourse into its plot, dramatis personae, etc." (Brummett, 1984b, p. 5). The third criterion requires that the anecdote must be synecdochic (Burke, 1969a, p. 326). It is a "summation" (Burke, 1969a, p. 60), a synecdochic reduction that contains the fundamental symbols of the essential dramatic conflict embodied in the larger discourse (Conrad, 1981, p. 46; Crable, 2000, pp. 323–324). The critic would relate "all incidents" of the discourse "to *one* organizing principle that prevails throughout the diversity of detail" [emphasis in original] (Burke, 1969a, p. 259).

King's speech obviously meets the first criterion for representativeness in that it is a symbolic act. The second and third criteria are scope and synecdoche. The representative anecdote must have scope in that it is "supple and complex enough" to be representative of the entire discourse under study, yet it must also be reductive "in that it is broadly a reduction of the subject matter" (Burke, 1969a, p. 60). In other words, it must synecdochically contain the essential elements of the discourse. "I Have a Dream" serves well as a representative anecdote for the first phase of the civil rights movement. The speech is the summation of the movement's goals articulated by its chief moderate spokesman. It is an extremely condensed piece of discourse which synecdochically presents the narrative of a nation founded upon the promise of freedom and democracy, the failure of the nation to live up to that promise "insofar as her citizens of color are concerned," and the future redemption of the nation through the extension of that promise to all its people. In other words, it symbolically enacts, from inception to resolution, the dramatic conflict between justice and injustice for African Americans. The speech is a sociodrama between good and bad, with good winning in the end. Furthermore, the speech is a compact distillation of King's thought. Except for the check/promissory note metaphor (see chapter 5), there was actually very little new material in the "Dream" speech. As I will demonstrate, the speech essentially restated ideas that were basic, recurring themes of King's rhetoric. These *topoi*, often in the same language, can be found in speeches and writings dating back as far as the beginning of King's public career (see chapter 2). After examining King's speeches to various audiences over the course of his career, Lucaites and Condit (1990) concluded "that 'I Have a Dream' is truly representative of King's rhetoric" (p. 21, n. 7). Dyson (2000) says that the speech was "the characteristic statement of King's career" (p. 17).

GUILT-PURIFICATION-REDEMPTION

This book argues that the underlying message/form, the representative anecdote, of King's "I Have a Dream" speech is a symbolic enactment of Burke's guilt-purification-redemption drama. Burke's redemption drama is a secular version of the Christian drama of sinful humans achieving salvation through the atoning sacrifice of Christ. This form is especially applicable to the rhetoric and ideas of King, a Christian preacher who became a secular spokesperson. Burke (1968a) noted that "form is a way of experiencing" in which the mind follows a process "amenable to it" (p. 143). Thus, "form is the creation of an appetite in the mind of the auditor, and the adequate satisfying of that appetite" (Burke, 1968a, p. 31). Therefore, the guilt-purification-redemption form allowed King to serve his ends of getting whites to accept equal justice for blacks by arousing their latent guilt and then providing them with a way to expiate that guilt. (King often spoke of the strategic importance of arousing the conscience of and establishing a sense of guilt in white America. See Clark, 1963, p. 42; M. L. King, 1986, p. 358.) It is an exchange in which whites provide socioeconomic justice for blacks in return for black absolution of white guilt. This exchange allows blacks to maintain dignity by giving something they have more of than whites (moral authority) for something whites have more of than blacks (socioeconomic-political authority). King had adopted an idea common in Judeo-Christian thought, but especially salient for American blacks because of their shared experience of slavery and discrimination; that is, that the history of suffering and oppression endured by African Americans had, in a sense, purified them, made them more morally virtuous than their oppressors, and had thus provided African Americans with a Christlike mission to redeem their oppressors (Cone, 1986, p. 26; Fullinwider, 1969; M. L. King, 1958, p. 63; Oates, 1982, p. 290). (This theme is developed more fully in chapter 4.) The motto of King's organization, the Southern Christian Leadership Conference (SCLC), was "To Redeem the Soul of America" (Fairclough, 1987, p. 32). King often said that the goal of the civil rights movement should be "redemption and reconciliation" (M. L. King, 1957a, p. 30; 1958, p. 102; 1986, p. 8), and his vision of the redeemed society, which he called "the beloved community," was "the organizing principle of all of King's thought and activity" (Smith and Zepp, 1974, p. 119).

Burke's redemption drama is a much overlooked aspect of his dramatistic theory. Burke does not actually present the full-blown theory *in toto* anywhere in his writings, but aspects of the theory are spread throughout most of his major works. Foss, Foss, and Trapp (1985) brought together the strands of the theory in their overview of Burke's ideas (pp. 178–182), and Rueckert's (1982) study of Burke discussed the theory as well (pp. 46–47, 104–109, 133–134). Duncan's (1962) review of Burke's dramatistic theory contained a discussion of Burke's concept of redemption through victimage (pp. 121–135).

There have been some previous applications of the guilt-purification-redemption model. Burke's (1973) study of Hitler's *Mein Kampf* demonstrated how Hitler used the Jews as scapegoats in promising German redemption (pp. 191–220). Brummett (1981) has examined how certain Burkean modes of purification—scapegoating, mortification, and transcendence—are manifested in some examples of presidential campaign rhetoric. Elwood (1989) demonstrated how *Philip Morris Magazine* uses dramas employing victimage and mortification to purge smokers of their guilt over smoking. Mechling and Mechling (1983) argue that the antisugar discourse of the 1970s moves through a pollution-guilt-purification-redemption scenario in which purification is effected through mortification and victimage. Scheibel (2002) uses the model to analyze the narrative of a guitar repairman. Williamson (2002) argues that the "Dragging Trial" of the white men convicted of dragging to death a black man in Jasper, Texas, served a purificatory function for the community. Only one study I am aware of has applied this theory to the rhetoric of Martin Luther King.

In her study of King's "Eulogy for the Martyred Children," a speech eulogizing the girls killed in the bombing of the Sixteenth Street Baptist Church in Birmingham, Alabama, only a few weeks after the March on Washington, Orr (1990) argues that King portrayed the girls as martyrs who died in a holy crusade, making their death an act of victimage for the purpose of redeeming the South and giving birth to a new order.

Generally, Burke's theory has been seen as offering two primary means of purifying guilt: victimage and mortification (Brock, 1980, p. 351; Foss, Foss, and Trapp, 1985, p. 180; Rueckert, 1982, p. 146). While Burke never says these are the only means of achieving purification, he usually cites one or the other as the means of absolving guilt, and often treats victimage and mortification as a pair (Burke, 1966, pp. 435, 478; 1970, pp. 190, 223, 248). Most of the studies reviewed above discuss redemption as taking place through victimage and/or mortification. Other Burkean means of symbolic purification—purification through transcendence and through images of change, movement, and dramatic catharsis—have been almost totally ignored by rhetorical critics. This book identifies King's use of purificatory images of change, movement, and dramatic catharsis, but the most important mode of purification in King's speech is transcendence. Therefore, one purpose of this book will be to develop and apply the theory of purification through transcendence.

METAPHORIC ANALYSIS

One other critical method, metaphoric analysis, will also be employed. King's speech is dense in metaphor. In order to attain a proper understanding of the speech, and to see how King's choice of metaphors contributes to his larger dramatic enactment, his metaphors must be studied. Therefore, chapter 5 uses contemporary metaphoric theory to analyze King's metaphors for the meaning they bring to the text and to demonstrate how they reinforce the guilt-purification-redemption form. Since an analysis of a social drama should seek to determine the role the discourse assigns to audience members as actors in the drama (Duncan, 1968, pp. 161–162), I also employ the concept of "the second persona." In his essay on the second persona, Edwin Black (1970) maintained that audiences "look to the discourse they are attending for cues that tell them how they are to view the world." A speaker's choice of metaphors can provide indications about the role the discourse provides for the audience (pp. 113, 119). An analysis of how King's metaphors constitute the audience as actors in the social drama of the civil rights movement will reveal a pattern of metaphorical meaning that reinforces King's use of transcendence and secular/religious mythology.

2

Agent and Scene

In order to fully understand the "I Have a Dream" speech it is necessary to understand the major intellectual influences on King's thought. King's philosophy and theology developed from a merging of the black church tradition with white Protestant liberalism. The "I Have a Dream" speech reflects these influences. Much of the speech, especially the "dream" sequence, is a rearticulation of ideas King had been expressing since early in his public career. Also, an understanding of the historical, intermediate, and immediate scene in which King's speech took place is essential to placing the speech in context and establishing its role as the representative anecdote of the first phase of the civil rights movement.

INTELLECTUAL INFLUENCES

Most early studies of King's thinking emphasized the influence of Protestant liberalism—especially the social gospel and personalism that King was exposed to in his graduate studies at Crozer Theological Seminary and Boston University—and the influence of Gandhian nonviolence (Ansbro, 1982; D. H. Smith, 1970; Smith and Zepp, 1974). However, later scholarship has acknowledged the early and central role of the black Southern Baptist church tradition in shaping King's ideas (Baldwin, 1984–1985; Cone, 1984, 1986; Dyson, 2000, pp. 123–130; Miller, 1992, 1993). The influences of liberal Protestant theology and Western philosophy gave "respectable" intellectual underpinnings to a worldview first nurtured in the biblically based black church tradition, and gave King the vocabulary to translate black theology to white America (Garrow, 1986b; Lischer, 1995, pp. 4–7; Miller, 1992, pp. 58–66).

Due to African Americans' history of slavery and oppression, in 1963 the black church had not yet developed a systematic theology as could be found in the white Christian tradition. Instead, black theology was manifested in sermons, songs, and the stories of slavery and oppression (Cone, 1984, p. 417). The central theme of black theology was the hope of freedom and reconciliation into a community of goodwill (Cone, 1984; Garber, 1974–1975). King called this the "Beloved Community," saw it as synonymous with the Kingdom of God, and depicted it in his theme of the "dream" (Cartwright, 1989; Cone, 1986, p. 22; Zepp, 1989, pp. 207–220). The African American religious tradition has also emphasized the dignity and worth of all human beings, and has seen God as a personal and loving God who takes an interest in the plight of His children (Baldwin, 1984–1985, pp. 98–101; also, see M. L. King, 1981, p. 83). When King encountered the social gospel of Walter Rauschenbusch and the theology of personalism in his graduate studies, he discovered the theological justification for the Beloved Community in the tradition of white Protestant liberalism. When combined with the American democratic tradition of equality, freedom, and justice, King's vision of the Beloved Community achieved a religious/secular synthesis with strong appeal to Americans of all races and religions.

King acknowledged the influence on his thinking of the social gospel of Walter Rauschenbusch (M. L. King, 1958, p. 91; 1986, pp. 345–346; also, see Lischer, 1995, pp. 54–55; and Morone, 2002, pp. 18–19, 416–417). The social gospel was a reaction to the stress on individual morality and redemption in orthodox American Protestantism of the late nineteenth and early twentieth centuries. Rauschenbusch argued that individualistic theology undervalued the social role and responsibility of religion. He taught that the Kingdom of God is collective, and that the individual is redeemed through participation in a redeemed and moral social order, which he termed the "beloved community" (Rauschenbusch, 1907, pp. 67–70; 1960, pp. 126–127). Rauschenbusch (1907) stressed the importance of the Old Testament prophets as exemplars of this view of religion because of their emphasis on public, as opposed to private, morality, and their sympathy with the oppressed (pp. 1–44). The Old Testament prophets sought "the social redemption of the nation" (Rauschenbusch, 1960, p. 24).

King's speeches and writings abound with references to the prophets. He extolled Amos, Hosea, Isaiah, and Jeremiah for speaking out against injustice and oppression (Ansbro, 1982, p. 166). His favorite prophet was Amos, whose line "But let judgment run down as waters, and righteousness as a mighty stream" (Amos 5:24) King used often in his own speeches (1957b; 1963a; 1986, p. 216), including the "I Have a Dream" speech. The "Dream" speech also incorporated a line from Isaiah (40:4) when King described his "dream that one day every valley shall be exalted, every hill and mountain shall be made low, the rough places will be made plain and the crooked places will be made straight, and the glory of the Lord shall be revealed, and all flesh shall see it together" (1963d, pp. 725–726). In his "Letter from Birmingham City Jail," King (1986) compared his own mission to that of the Old Testament prophets (p. 290). The influence of the idea of collective redemption permeates the "Dream" speech and is connected to the concept of the Beloved Community, which will be examined shortly, but earlier speeches by King also speak of the need for the "salvation of the world" (1957b) and the "salvation of our civilization" (1957a, p. 30).

The other major school of thought from white Protestant liberalism that King embraced was personalism. King chose Boston University for his doctoral studies because with Edgar Brightman, Harold DeWolf, and others, it was the center for the study of personalism, to which King was initially exposed under George Davis at Crozer (Garrow, 1986b, p. 12; Lischer, 1995, pp. 57–60). Personalism holds that conscious personality is the supreme value and supreme reality in the universe. The universe is seen as an organic whole, an interacting system of persons with the central and supreme personality being God. All persons are imperfect copies of the Supreme Personality, yet they have inherent dignity and worth because they participate in the ultimate reality of God (Ansbro, 1982, p. 287; Smith and Zepp, 1974, pp. 100–101; Warren, 2001, pp. 120–121). Thus, the central tenet of personalism—the intrinsic value of all individuals—King found attractive because it had consonance with and provided "intellectual" justification for the same theme in black theology (Garrow, 1986b, pp. 12–13; Miller 1992, p. 62). King (1958) described personalism as his "basic philosophical position" and said that "it gave metaphysical and philosophical grounding for the idea of a personal God, and it gave me a metaphysical basis for the dignity and worth of all human personality" (p. 100). Personalism provided King with the philosophical basis for his attack on segregation (Smith and Zepp, 1974, p. 106) and its influence is evident in King's rhetoric. He told the audience at the First Annual Institute on Nonviolence and Social Change, "Whatever affects one directly affects all indirectly. We are all links in the great chain of humanity," (M. L. King, 1957a, p. 28); and in a 1961 speech he said: "all life is interrelated. We are caught in an inescapable network of mutuality; tied in a single garment of destiny. Whatever affects one directly, affects all indirectly" (M. L. King, 1986, p. 209; also, see M. L. King, 1981, p. 70). The same theme appears in the "Dream" speech, where King tells his followers that many white people "have come to realize that their destiny is tied up with our destiny. And they have come to realize that their freedom is inextricably bound to our freedom" (M. L. King, 1963d, p. 724). Because all human beings are related, life is social, and because all humans partake, although imperfectly, of the essence of a loving and moral God, they have the capacity for moral improvement. Thus, for the personalists the goal of human existence is the creation of a loving and moral society (Smith and Zepp, 1974, pp. 107–114).

The black religious tradition of the hope for freedom and reconciliation, the social gospel of Rauschenbusch, and the theology of personalism, all converged in King's concept of the Beloved Community. While King spoke of the Beloved Community often (M. L. King, 1957a, p. 30; 1958, p. 102; 1986, p. 8), he never defines it in detail. An early SCLC brochure simply states: "The ultimate aim of SCLC is to foster and create the 'beloved community' in America where brotherhood is a reality. . . . Our ultimate goal is genuine intergroup and interpersonal living—*integration*" [emphasis in original] (This is SCLC, n.d.). Ansbro (1982) describes King's concept of the Beloved Community as a society based on *agape* (love) in all social relations, where discrimination is excluded and each person is regarded in the image of God (pp. 187–188). Cartwright (1989) states that for King the Beloved Community is virtually synonymous with the Kingdom of God and is depicted in the "dream" theme (pp. 3–5). Smith and Zepp (1974) describe it as a "transformed and regenerated human society" where "brotherhood would be an actuality in every aspect of social life" (p. 120). They claim that the Beloved Community is grounded in the scriptural view of the millennial hope of the Kingdom of God and was closely related to the American democratic ideal of a nation of justice, equality, and freedom (pp. 125–131).

While King does not actually provide a definition of the Beloved Community, it is depicted in numerous speeches as the goal of the civil rights movement. In his 1956 address to the First Annual Institute on Nonviolence and Social Change, King describes:

> a new world in which men will live together as brothers; a world in which men will beat their swords into ploughshares and their spears into pruning-hooks; a world in which men will no longer take necessities from the masses to give luxuries to the classes; a world in which all men will respect the dignity and worth of all human personality. (M. L. King, 1957a, p. 34)

In a speech at the Highlander Folk School, King (1957b) spoke of the "*dream* of the Fatherhood of God and the Brotherhood of Man" [emphasis added]. In what is apparently one of the earliest elaborations of the dream motif, in a 1960 speech to the National Urban League, King concluded by calling upon his audience to work to rid the body politic of

> this cancerous disease of discrimination which is preventing our democratic and Christian health from being realized. Then and only then will we be able to bring

> into full realization the dream of our American democracy—a dream yet unfulfilled. A dream of equality of opportunity, of privilege and property widely distributed . . . a dream of a land where men do not argue that the color of a man's skin determines the content of his character . . . the dream of a country where every man will respect the dignity and worth of all human personality, and men will dare to live together as brothers—that is the dream. (M. L. King, 1986, pp. 150–151)

In a 1961 commencement address at Lincoln University in Pennsylvania, titled "The American Dream," King told his audience:

> I should like to discuss with you some aspects of the American dream. For in a real sense, America is essentially a dream, a dream as yet unfulfilled. It is a dream of a land where men of all races, of all nationalities and of all creeds can live together as brothers. The substance of the dream is expressed in these sublime words, words lifted to cosmic proportions: "We hold these truths to be self-evident, that all men are created equal, that they are endowed by their Creator with certain unalienable rights, that among these are life, liberty, and the pursuit of happiness." This is the dream. (M. L. King, 1986, p. 208)

King was obviously evolving toward the wording of the dream sequence that would stir the nation at the March on Washington. He used the dream motif in wording similar to that in the 1960 National Urban League speech cited above, at a December 1961 speech before the AFL-CIO, and a July 1962 address at the National Press Club (M. L. King, 1986, pp. 105, 206). He used it again in Birmingham in April 1963 (Fairclough, 1987, p. 155). On June 23, 1963, at a Detroit rally attended by 125,000 people, King spoke to the largest crowd he had ever addressed up to that time (Branch, 1988, p. 843). He employed much of the phraseology he would use later that summer in his most famous speech, such as the "Now is the time" refrain and the line about "transform[ing] the dangling [*sic*] discords of our nation into a beautiful symphony of brotherhood" (M. L. King, 1963a). In his peroration King delivered his latest rendering of the dream motif. This rendering is longer than, and lacks the succinct vividness of, the version delivered on August 28, but it demonstrates how King was gradually refining this theme:

> And so this afternoon, I have a dream. It is a dream deeply rooted in the American dream. I have a dream that one day, right down in Georgia and Mississippi and Alabama, the sons of former slaves and the sons of former slave owners will be able to live together as brothers.
>
> I have a dream this afternoon, that one day . . . that one day little white children and little Negro children will be able to join hands as brothers and sisters.
>
> I have a dream this afternoon that one day, that one day men will no longer burn down houses and the church of God simply because people want to be free.

> I have a dream this afternoon that there will be a day when we will no longer face the atrocities that Emmett Till had to face or Medgar Evers had to face. That all men can live with dignity.
>
> I have a dream this afternoon that my four little children . . . that my four little children will not come up in the same young days that I came up within. That they will be judged on the basis of the content of their character, not the color of their skin.
>
> I have a dream this afternoon that one day, right here in Detroit, Negroes will be able to buy a house or rent a house anywhere that their money will carry them and they will be able to get a job.
>
> I have a dream this afternoon!
>
> I have a dream that one day "every valley shall be exalted and every hill and mountain shall be made low. The rough places will be made plain and the crooked places will be made straight, and the glory of the Lord shall be revealed, and all flesh shall see it together."
>
> I have a dream this afternoon that the brotherhood of man will become a reality in this day. And with this faith I will go out and carve a tunnel of hope through the mountain of despair. With this faith, I will go with you and transform dark yesterdays into bright tomorrows. With this faith we will be able to achieve this new day when all of God's children, black men and white men, Jews and Gentiles, protestants and Catholics, will be able to join hands and sing with the Negro in the spiritual of old: "Free at last. Free at last. Thank God Almighty, we are free at last." (M. L. King, 1963a)

King had used the "Free at last" conclusion before (1986, pp. 207, 216) and he would use it again in the "I Have a Dream" speech. The merging of scripture, song lyrics, and excerpts from traditional sermons into one's own sermon was a common practice in the black folk pulpit tradition (Miller 1988, 1989). We saw above that King often embedded scripture from Amos and Isaiah into his speeches. He had merged Jefferson's most famous line from the Declaration of Independence, "We hold these truths to be self-evident" into his speeches before (1957b; 1986, p. 208) and did so again in the "Dream" speech (1963d, p. 725). The use of song lyrics from "America the Beautiful" ("My country 'tis of thee") followed by the "Let freedom ring" refrain which he uses near the end of "I Have a Dream" (1963d, p. 726), had also been used before by King (1957a, p. 34). Miller (1989) points out that this was adapted from a similar peroration by Archibald Carey in an address to the 1952 Republican National Convention (pp. 28–29).

In sum, King's thinking reflected a merging of the ideas of the black church tradition with the theology of white Protestant liberalism. In the theology of the social gospel and personalism he found the "intellectual justification" he needed to translate the African American religious themes of freedom and reconciliation into the community, and the concept of God as a personal and loving Being who values the dignity and worth of each human being, into terms acceptable to white Protestant America. These themes culminated in King's vision of the redeemed and integrated society, which he called the "Beloved Community." These ideas, as reflected in the "I Have a Dream" speech, were recurrent *topoi* of King's rhetoric going back to the early years of his public career.

THE SCENE—MARCH ON WASHINGTON

The event at which King's "I Have a Dream" speech took place was the March on Washington on August 28, 1963. The March on Washington was a long-planned and much anticipated event which was the culmination of a series of civil rights activities that took place in the spring and summer of 1963, and which, in a larger sense, the civil rights movement had been working toward for decades. It was probably the high point of the civil rights movement, as well as of King's career. Its overwhelming success in gathering several hundred thousand people, both black and white, for a peaceful demonstration for civil rights has marked it as a defining event of the movement, of which King's speech was the climactic moment. In order to put the event, and King's speech, into context I will describe the scene in three parts: (1) the historical scene, which briefly chronicles the history and tradition of protest marches on the nation's capital and outlines the history of marches in Washington for black civil rights prior to the 1963 march; (2) the intermediate scene, which describes the events of the spring and summer of 1963 leading up to the March on Washington; and (3) the immediate scene, which describes the March on Washington itself in order to provide an understanding of the setting in which King's speech took place.

The tradition of exercising the constitutional "right of the people peaceably to assemble, and to petition the government for a redress of grievances" goes back to the earliest days of the nation. In 1783 unpaid soldiers marched to Philadelphia, at that time the nation's capital, to demand salaries due them from the fledgling and impecunious government. In 1894, a time of high unemployment and depression, Jacob Coxey led about 400 people from Ohio to Washington, D.C., to demand public works programs and a "legal tender" bill designed to put unbacked paper money into circulation. Mounted police dispersed the demonstrators and Coxey was jailed. Five thousand suffragettes marched down Pennsylvania Avenue in 1913, and in 1925 the Ku Klux Klan staged a march and held a ceremony at the Washington Monument in which 25,000 people turned out. In June of 1932, during the Great Depression, the army was used to remove 20,000 World War I veterans, known as the Bonus

Army, who refused to leave after descending upon Washington to demand immediate payment of bonuses authorized by Congress in 1924, but not due until 1945. A series of smaller marches by the unemployed and hungry were staged in Washington over the next eleven months. In May of 1933 a second Bonus Army was received more warmly by the new Roosevelt administration and left town without incident. The bonus payment was finally authorized in 1936 (Gentile, 1983, pp. 82–86).

The idea of using a march in the nation's capital to petition for the rights of African Americans was the brainchild of A. Philip Randolph, the black labor leader. In September of 1940, Randolph, Walter White of the NAACP, and T. Arnold Hill of the National Urban League met with President Roosevelt to protest the segregation of blacks in the armed forces and the lack of access by blacks to most jobs in defense industries. After several months went by and it became apparent that the meeting had not produced any action on Roosevelt's part, Randolph began organizing and planning a march of 10,000 blacks down Pennsylvania Avenue to demand jobs in defense industries and integration of the armed forces. Encouraged by the favorable reaction of the black community, Randolph eventually raised his estimate to 100,000 marchers. Shocked and frightened by the prospect of 100,000 black people marching in the nation's capital, Roosevelt asked Randolph to call off the march. Randolph refused to do so without a tangible concession in return. Finally, Roosevelt issued an executive order creating the Fair Employment Practices Committee (FEPC) that improved job opportunities for blacks in the defense industry. In return, Randolph called off the march, but the preparations for the march had aroused a sense of activism in the black community, leaving many discontented and charging that Randolph had "sold out." Randolph responded that the main goal of the march, jobs in defense industries, had been achieved and that the march was not really canceled, only "postponed." He told the black community that the threat of a march was "our ace in the hole" to make sure the government kept its commitment. To appease his critics and to keep the threat alive, Randolph formed the March on Washington Movement (MOWM) from the march organization he had built. The MOWM held a series of rallies and conferences around the country in the early forties, and although it did keep alive for a time the threat of a mass march on Washington, its activities subsided after 1943 and it died out by the late forties (Pfeffer, 1990, pp. 45–55). The FEPC, which faced stringent opposition in Congress every year when it came up for renewal, was finally eliminated in 1946 (Graham, 1990, pp. 9–14).

Although Randolph's plan for a huge march did not materialize until 1963, a series of smaller civil rights demonstrations took place in Washington in the late fifties. The first, the Prayer Pilgrimage for Freedom, was held at the Lincoln Memorial on May 17, 1957, to commemorate the third anniversary of the Supreme Court's *Brown v. Board of Education* decision. It was organized by Randolph, King, and Roy Wilkins of the NAACP, all of who spoke at the rally. Its objectives were to protest violent resistance to integration in the South and legal harassment of the NAACP by some southern state governments, as well as to demonstrate support for passage of the civil rights legislation, essentially a voting rights bill, then pending in Congress. Despite the sponsors' predictions that 50,000 to 75,000 people would attend, only 15,000 to 25,000 showed up and the event garnered little media attention (Garrow, 1986a, pp. 92–94). The Prayer Pilgrimage is mainly remembered as a precursor to the much more successful March on Washington six years later, and as marking the ascension of King, whose "Give Us the Ballot" speech received the most enthusiastic response of the day, to national prominence as a civil rights spokesman on par with Randolph and Wilkins (Pfeffer, 1990, p. 179). Although the event probably had little influence, Congress did pass the 1957 Civil Rights Act, but it was so watered down it had slight effect (Dallek, 2003, pp. 214–217; Graham, 1990, p. 23). In October 1958 the first Youth March for Integrated Schools was held; a second, which drew about 22,000, was held in 1959. King did not attend the first of these because he was recuperating from a stabbing incident that had occurred in September of 1958, but he did address the 1959 march, urging the youth to "Commit yourself to the noble struggle for equal rights. You will make a greater person of yourself, a greater nation of your country, and a finer world to live in" (M. L. King, 1986, p. 22). Although these civil rights demonstrations of the late fifties had little substantive effect, Pfeffer (1990) argues that they did impress the white community with the peaceful and dignified manner in which they were handled and that they had a profound emotional impact on the participants who became excited with the potential of using mass marches to demonstrate for their rights (pp. 199–200).

In late 1962, in order to draw public attention to the need for more jobs for African Americans and to call for a broad-based program to insure economic justice, Randolph began discussing the possibility of revising his march proposal of the 1940s. He asked Bayard Rustin, who had handled the details of organizing the marches in the late fifties, to prepare a memo outlining tentative plans for such an action. Initial plans called for a two-day "mass descent" upon Washington in June of 1963. On the first day, mass sit-ins would take place at Capitol Hill, blocking all normal congressional business, while a smaller delegation visited the White House. Both Congress and the president would be presented with detailed legislative demands. On the second day a mass procession down Pennsylvania Avenue would be followed by a rally at the Lincoln Memorial. On March 23, 1963, Randolph presented the plan to the executive board of his Negro American Labor Council (NALC), which readily approved it. During March and April Randolph and Rustin attempted to interest the other civil rights organizations in the plan and the march was rescheduled for October to allow time to gather support and make preparations. In order to obtain the participation of the more radical activists at SNCC and CORE, Rustin emphasized that there would be mass sit-ins designed to disrupt government business. This part of the plan was later jettisoned, prompting charges of a "sellout" from more radical blacks such as Malcolm X and James Forman of SNCC (Forman, 1972, pp. 335–336; Malcolm X, 1965, pp. 14–17). When Randolph contacted National Urban League director Whitney Young and the NAACP's Roy Wilkins about supporting the march, they both demurred because of their aversion to civil disobedience. King and the SCLC were also little interested at this time because they were preoccupied with the direct action campaign they had just begun in Birmingham, Alabama. Randolph and Rustin kept the plan on the front burner, but little progress was made that spring (Garrow, 1986a, pp. 266–267; Pfeffer, 1990, pp. 240–241).

Although it is probably an exaggeration to say, as King did later, that "without Birmingham, the march on Washington wouldn't have been called" (M. L. King, 1986, p. 351), the Birmingham campaign in the spring of 1963 did provide the momentum which propelled the civil rights organizations toward the March on Washington. It was Birmingham, more than any other event, that brought to the nation's attention what the media that year came to call "the Negro revolution." Lentz (1990) called Birmingham "the pivotal event of the black movement" (p. 294) that, along with the March on Washington, "stamped Martin Luther King as a symbol on the consciousness of America" (p. 75). Before Birmingham, King was one of several major civil rights leaders. After Birmingham, he was, as a *Newsweek* poll found that summer, the top civil rights leader in the eyes of black America ("The Big Man Is," 1963). Birmingham and the March on Washington achieved such symbolic importance because the events reverberated against each other, providing the antithesis of confrontation and consensus, and the contrasting images of Bull Connor as the personification of evil and King as the moral leader of the nation (Lentz 1990, p. 76).

Birmingham was the most carefully crafted direct action campaign King and the SCLC had undertaken to date.[1] After the failure of their Albany, Georgia, campaign in 1961–1962, King and his aides realized that if their nonviolent direct action did not elicit violent overreaction from police or sheriff's deputies, the media soon lost interest and public sympathy swung to the governmental authorities (Fairclough, 1987, pp. 107–109; Garrow, 1978, pp. 2–3, 220–231; 1986a, pp. 216–217; Lischer, 1995, pp. 157–158; Rorabaugh, 2002, pp. 104–105). Birmingham was chosen because it was a bastion of southern segregation, because the local leader, the Reverend Fred Shuttlesworth, had built a strong organization, but especially because Police Commissioner Eugene "Bull" Connor had a reputation for short-tempered violence. The campaign, which consisted of boycotts, sit-ins, demonstrations, and marches, commenced on April 3, but did not begin well for King and the SCLC. Many local leaders—both white and black—the national media, and the Kennedy administration criticized the timing of the campaign. Because a new city government under the more moderate Albert Boutwell was due to soon take office, many felt the SCLC should wait to see if the new government would be willing to accept many of the SCLC's demands without the need for demonstrations. Also, Connor, who was challenging Boutwell's election in court, showed uncharacteristic restraint by refraining from the use of violence when making arrests. After nine days of demonstrations with no tangible results, the spirits of local blacks began to sag and the media was losing interest. In an attempt to inspire his followers and ignite publicity, King defied a court injunction and led a march on Good Friday, April 12. He was in jail eight days, during which time he wrote the now famous "Letter from Birmingham City Jail," although the letter received little notice at the time.

King's arrest temporarily rekindled interest, but by the end of April the demonstrators' spirits were sagging again and the campaign organizers were running out of people willing to march. By not using violence on the marchers Connor was depriving the movement of the drama it needed to generate publicity and sympathy. Finally, King made the crucial decision his aides had been urging upon him; he agreed to allow high school and grade school children to march. On Thursday, May 2, wave after wave of children left the Sixteenth Street Baptist Church heading toward downtown Birmingham. More than 500 young marchers were arrested that day and the Birmingham campaign was back in the news. When hundreds more youngsters marched on May 3, Connor made the fateful decision to use police dogs and fire hoses to break up the march. The newspaper photographs and television images of snarling police dogs and powerful fire hoses unleashed upon young black marchers seared the conscience of the nation and the world. The confrontation continued being played out in front of the cameras, and by Monday, May 6, more than 3,000 black people were in Birmingham jails—the largest number ever imprisoned at one time in the history of the movement—and thousands more were still demonstrating. Daily pictures of police brutality against black marchers were shocking the nation and winning widespread public sympathy for the civil rights movement. With its jails full and its national reputation disgraced, Birmingham's more moderate civic and business leaders called for accommodation. On May 8 the SCLC suspended its demonstrations and on May 10 a desegregation agreement was reached.

After the success of Birmingham, King was searching for a way to capitalize on the publicity and sympathy that had been generated for the civil rights movement. He was disappointed with President Kennedy's meager actions thus far in the area of civil rights. By the end of May King was discussing with aides the possibility of calling for a mass "March on Washington," which might include sit-ins on Capitol Hill, to pressure the president and Congress to act on the behalf of civil rights for African Americans. Impelled by the national outrage over Birmingham, and the wave of civil rights demonstrations across the country inspired by the Birmingham example, the Kennedy administration was privately considering initiating civil rights legislation. Meanwhile, Alabama governor George Wallace was threatening to disobey a court order requiring the admission of two black students to the University of Alabama. The Alabama crisis peaked on June 11 when Wallace made his famous, though largely symbolic, stand in the schoolhouse door. The president federalized the Alabama National Guard and Wallace stood aside when the commanding general ordered him to do so later that same day, and the black students were admitted. That evening, Kennedy went on national television and announced that he would soon send to Congress a civil rights bill that included a public accommodations section. He told the nation "We are confronted primarily with a moral issue. It is as old as the Scriptures and is as clear as the American Constitution. . . . Now is the time for this nation to fulfill its promise" (Heffner, 1985, pp. 330–331). The speech was Kennedy's first clear and unequivocal call for the elimination of racial discrimination in America. It marked the beginning of the federal government's full-scale commitment to end segregation (Branch, 1988, pp. 816–824; Garrow, 1986a, pp. 264–269; Goldzwig and Dionisopoulos, 1989, pp. 189–191; Rorabaugh, 2002, pp. 110–112).

King was extremely pleased with Kennedy's speech and decided that the thrust of the March on Washington should now be directed toward urging Congress to pass Kennedy's civil rights legislation. Since Randolph was still planning his march for jobs, King and Randolph decided to combine their two marches into one. On June 19 King and his advisers met with Randolph, Rustin, and representatives from SNCC and CORE for the first group discussion of the March on Washington. The NAACP and the NUL, not yet on board, were not represented. Randolph's economic goals and King's broader civil rights objectives were merged by calling the event the "March on Washington for Jobs and Freedom" and it was decided to aim for a date between August 10 and 24, designed to coincide with the expected Senate filibuster of Kennedy's bill. The march was announced to the press on June 21. The Kennedy administration, not pleased at the prospect of thousands of black protestors marching on Washington, summoned the black leadership to the

White House for a meeting the next day. Kennedy tried to convince the leaders that a march might backfire by giving the impression blacks were attempting to intimidate Congress. The black leaders responded by saying that the black masses were already in the streets demonstrating anyway, and that a peaceful march led by responsible leaders would be the best way to channel that legitimate discontent. The meeting ended with the black leadership holding firm and Kennedy still not fully convinced of the wisdom of the march (Garrow, 1986a, pp. 269–272; Pfeffer, 1990, p. 244).

Public reaction to the planned march was less than enthusiastic. The nation was in the throes of the "Negro revolution" and there was widespread concern that a large march in the nation's capital might turn violent. Birmingham had spawned a wave of black activism across the nation that even some civil rights leaders worried might get out of control ("Worried Leaders," 1963). By one estimate, in the ten-week period after the Birmingham desegregation settlement on May 10, there were 758 racial demonstrations in 186 American cities resulting in 14,733 arrests (Branch, 1988, p. 825). Many newspaper editorials criticized the planned march and a Gallup Poll found that 63 percent of all Americans had an "unfavorable" attitude toward it (Gentile, 1983, pp. 42–43). Fueling the concern were reports of remarks such as those by the Reverend George Lawrence, SCLC's New York director, who said that a mass sit-in in Washington and a national campaign of civil disobedience would ensue if a filibuster against Kennedy's bill was attempted ("Threats: Negroes' Latest Weapon," 1963, p. 39). King and Randolph realized, however, that massive civil disobedience would be counterproductive to the goal of passing the civil rights bill. They also realized that the full support of the NAACP, the largest and richest civil rights organization, was essential if the march was to be a success, and that the NAACP's director, Roy Wilkins, would never go along with a plan for massive civil disobedience. For his part, Wilkins knew that with other major civil rights leaders such as King and Randolph involved, he and the NAACP would look bad if they did not participate. On July 2 the crucial meeting of "the Big Six"—King, Randolph, Wilkins, Whitney Young of the National Urban League, James Farmer of CORE, and John Lewis of SNCC—was held. In exchange for Wilkins' support the earlier plans for massive sit-ins were officially scrapped. The march was now a one-day affair, to be held on August 28. The leaders emerged from the meeting assuring the media that the march would be a peaceful and orderly event (Branch, 1988, pp. 847–848; Gentile, 1983, pp. 41–42).

The march was further legitimized when major labor and religious organizations were brought aboard. The "Big Six" became "the Big Ten" with the addition of Walter Reuther, president of the United Auto Workers, Dr. Eugene Carson Blake of the United Presbyterian Church, Rabbi Joachim Prinz, president of the American Jewish Congress, and Matthew Ahmann, executive director of the National Catholic Conference for Interracial Justice (Pfeffer, 1990, p. 245). Meanwhile, the Kennedy administration, bowing to the inevitable, decided to cooperate with the march organizers to help assure a peaceful and orderly assembly that would not endanger the civil rights legislation. By mid-July the widespread concern over the march began to dissipate, and in a July 17 press conference the president publicly endorsed the march for the first time (Garrow, 1986a, p. 278; Rorabaugh, 2002, p. 120).

By early August most of the post-Birmingham activism had abated as that energy was now being put into the preparation for the march. After a hectic eleven weeks of personal appearances and march planning, King took a ten-day vacation in mid-August to rest and begin work on his book about the Birmingham campaign (Fairclough, 1987, pp. 141–149; Garrow, 1986a, p. 280). In the days immediately preceding the march the television and print media gave it extensive pre-event publicity. *Time*, *Newsweek*, *U.S. News and World Report*, *Life*, and most major newspapers carried prominent stories on the planned march, usually including a list of march demands, a schedule of the day's events, and a map showing the route the march would follow. The main march demands included passage of the civil rights bill, an end to segregation in the schools, and a federal program to train and employ all unemployed workers in "meaningful and dignified jobs at decent wages" ("The March in Washington," 1963). The march received cautious endorsement from *Life*, the *St. Louis Post-Dispatch*, the *New York Times*, and other major publications. The *Washington Post* editorialized that the march would be "a great demonstration of the ways of democracy" and expressed "confidence that it will be remembered as an outpouring of good will, understanding and tolerance" ("Washington on Stage," 1963).

Washington, D.C., on Wednesday, August 28, 1963, was clear and sunny with a high temperature in the low eighties. Most government employees had been given the day off to avoid congestion. The sale of alcohol in the District of Columbia was banned for the day. Because of concerns about the possibility of violence, 1900 regular policemen were on duty and all leaves had been canceled for the other 1,000 Washington police officers. Two thousand National Guardsmen were on duty in the area and the army was ready with 4,000 troops at nearby Fort Meyer and another 15,000 paratroopers at Fort Bragg, North Carolina, if needed. In addition, march organizers had arranged for 2,000 civilian "marshals," most of them off-duty, black police officers from New York, to be present (Gentile, 1983, pp. 139, 147–149; "All's Set for March," 1963).

Because it was one of the first major events transmitted live to Europe via the new Telestar satellite, the March on Washington received the most extensive worldwide TV coverage ever afforded up to that time. One thousand six hundred special press passes were issued, many to foreign correspondents, in addition to the 1,200 press passes already possessed by full-time Washington reporters. Thirty-five television cameras were employed to broadcast the event. CBS provided complete live coverage of the afternoon program at the Lincoln Memorial, with ABC and NBC providing periodic live reports and standing by to break in with live coverage as events warranted (Gentile, 1983, pp. 201–202, 222–223).

That morning, while the march leaders called upon members of Congress, marchers gathering at the Washington Monument were entertained by a program that included Joan Baez, Bob Dylan, and Peter, Paul, and Mary. Impatient to begin, the marchers left ten minutes ahead of schedule for the walk to the Lincoln Memorial and the march leaders had to be rushed to the scene to "lead" the march for the cameras. Estimates of the total attendance for the event ranged from 200,000 to 400,000 people, about one-fourth of who were white (Gentile, 1983, pp. 202–206, 229–230; Lewis, 1978, p. 224; Rorabaugh, 2002, p. 120).

Shortly after 1:00 P.M. the official program began with Camilla Williams singing the national anthem, followed by the invocation by the Very Reverend Patrick O'Boyle, archbishop of Washington. Each of the ten main speakers of the day was asked to limit his remarks to eight minutes in order to keep the program on schedule (all of the main speakers were male, although in a compromise with female civil rights activists, the organizers agreed to a segment of the program in which several prominent women in the movement would be introduced and allowed to briefly stand and acknowledge applause). The first speaker of the afternoon was Randolph. Stressing the economic theme, he told the crowd: "We are the advance guard of a massive moral revolution for jobs and freedom," and demanded "new forms of social planning to create full employment" ("Excerpts from," 1963). Reverend Dr. Eugene Carson Blake of the National Council of Churches criticized American churches for not coming out more forcefully in favor of black civil rights. John Lewis's speech "sent an electric charge" through the crowd (D. H. Smith, 1964, p. 193). Lewis, whose speech was toned down after O'Boyle and others objected to some of the harsh language in his prepared remarks, still gave the most incendiary speech of the day. He said that he supported the civil rights bill, but "with great reservations" because it did not do enough. He told his listeners "we are involved in a serious social revolution" and urged them to "get in and stay in the streets . . . until the unfinished revolution of 1776 is complete." He closed by promising that:

> If we do not get meaningful legislation out of this Congress, the time will come when we will not confine our marching to Washington. We will march through the South. . . . By the force of our demands . . . we shall splinter the segregated South into a thousand pieces and put them back together in the image of God and democracy. Wake up, America! (Forman, 1972, pp. 336–337)

Walter Reuther's speech drew crowd approval when he declared his support for civil rights "as a matter of human decency, as a matter of common morality." He said the rally was "the beginning of a great moral crusade to arouse America to the unfinished work of American democracy" (D. H. Smith, 1964, p. 194; *Congressional Record*, 1963, p. 16229). Roy Wilkins urged congressional approval of the civil rights bill and stressed the need to include "an FEPC bill as part of the package" (*Congressional Record*, 1963, p. 16229). It was after 3:00 P.M. when Wilkins finished and the long, hot day was beginning to take its toll on the crowd as many began to drift back to the buses that had brought them, but gospel singer Mahalia Jackson's rendition of "I've Been 'Buked and I've Been Scorned" reinvigorated the gathering (Gentile, 1983, p. 239). The lyrics of her spiritual helped set the stage for King's redemption drama:

> I'm gonna tell my Lord
> when I get home
> just how long you've
> been treating me wrong . . .
> I've been 'buked and I've been scorned
> Trying to make this journey all alone.

The next speaker, Rabbi Prinz, was the last before King, who was scheduled to give the final speech of the day. Prinz spoke of "the shame and disgrace of inequality and injustice which make a mockery of the great American idea" and identified the Jewish experience with the black experience (*Congressional Record*, 1963, p. 16228). After Prinz finished, some in the crowd, knowing from their program that King would be next, began to chant, "Martin Luther King, Martin Luther King." King, introduced by Randolph as "the moral leader of our nation," received a one-minute ovation from the crowd. ABC and NBC cut away from regular afternoon programming to join CBS in live coverage of King's speech. After the applause died down, King began speaking from his prepared text (Branch, 1988, p. 881; Gentile, 1983, p. 240).

NOTE

1. My account of the Birmingham campaign and its effect is taken from: Branch (1988, pp. 725–786); Dallek (2003, pp. 594–606); Garrow (1986a, pp. 236–264); Fairclough (1987, pp. 111–134); Oates (1982, pp. 215–238); and Rorabaugh (2002, pp. 105–112).

3

Act: The Redemption of the Audience's Guilt

King's "I Have a Dream" was a symbolic articulation of a redemption drama, played out on a national stage, in which the soul of America was at stake. King was very much aware of the audiences he had to appeal to and the potency of guilt as a factor in human motivation. As the leader of the most "conservative" of the direct action civil rights organizations, King occupied the "vital center" of the civil rights movement (Meier, 1965, p. 56). In his "Letter from Birmingham City Jail," King acknowledged his position in the strategic middle when he wrote: "I stand in the middle of two opposing forces in the Negro community. One is the force of complacency . . . the other force is one of bitterness and hatred, and comes perilously close to advocating violence" (M. L. King, 1986, p. 296). To King's left stood the more radical young activists at SNCC and CORE who thought King overly cautious, and to their left, others—represented chiefly by the Black Muslims and Malcolm X—who advocated even more rapid change through forceful and sometimes violent tactics. To King's right stood not only the older, more established civil rights organizations—the NAACP and the National Urban League—but most of white America. By 1963 "massive resistance" to desegregation had largely broken down, and the issue had become one of the proper timing of the steps toward integration, with white moderates advocating a policy of "gradualism" (see Cox, 1989, pp. 184–187). Thus, King in addressing a national audience was really addressing two major audiences with conflicting viewpoints. He had "to persuade whites that they should not countenance gradualism and to persuade blacks that they should not pursue radical change" (Hariman, 1989, p. 210).

That King had these two audiences in mind is clear from his prepared remarks which emphasized America's long overdue obligation to her black citizens, while cautioning blacks against extremism and violence (see M. L. King, 1963b).

From his prepared text, King spoke on the theme of America's failure to live up to its "promissory note" to provide "the unalienable rights of life, liberty, and the pursuit of happiness" to its people of color. He stressed "the fierce urgency of now" and warned against the "tranquilizing drug of gradualism." Then, turning to his black audience, King cautioned African Americans not to resort to hatred and violence in their struggle to gain their legitimate rights: "In the process of gaining our rightful place we must not be guilty of wrongful deeds. Let us not seek to satisfy our thirst for freedom by drinking from the cup of bitterness and hatred" (M. L. King, 1963b; 1963d, p. 724). While King's prepared remarks address his two major audiences separately, his extemporized remarks, the words he uttered from the "dream" sequence to the end of the speech, unite those audiences by transcending their differences. As he was nearing the end of his prepared speech, caught up in the crowd response to his words, King abandoned his script and extemporized the words that electrified the crowd and forever stamped him as a national symbol (Branch, 1988, p. 882; Garrow, 1986a, p. 283; D. H. Smith, 1964, p. 221).

It is reported that some people were crying at the conclusion of King's address ("Biggest Protest March," 1963; D. H. Smith, 1964, pp. 223–224). One participant described his response this way:

> [I]t just seemed to move you off the platform, off the earth . . . Dr. King brought to life the hope that someday we could walk together hand in hand. . . . It was a matter of being inspired and moved. It was an awfully sentimental and spiritual experience for me. (Hampton and Fayer, 1990, p. 168)

The speech was widely commented upon and excerpted in news accounts of the march. In the *New York Times*, James Reston (1963) wrote that until King spoke "the pilgrimage was merely a great spectacle," but King "brought them alive with a peroration that was an anguished echo from all the old American reformers" (p. 1). Marquis W. Childs (1963), writing in the *St. Louis Post-Dispatch*, said that King's speech "rose above mere oratory to a moving peroration of what the future can mean for an America that has wiped out the hatred of race prejudice" (p. 20 D). Eugene Patterson (1963) of the *Atlanta Constitution* praised King's powerful "vision of brotherhood and plenty" (pp. 1, 14).

The long-term assessment of the speech has marked it as "one of history's greatest public addresses" (O'Brien, 1988, p. 49). Leff (1987) calls it "an established classic." Boulware (1969) compares its significance to Lincoln's "Gettysburg Address" and William Jennings Bryan's "Cross of Gold" speech

(p. 252). Dyson (2000) declares it to be "the defining oration of our age" (p. 17) and 137 scholars of American public address voted it the most significant American political speech of the twentieth century (American Rhetoric, Top 100 Speeches, 2002).

REDEMPTION DRAMA

What accounts for this speech's immediate effect on the audience and its long-term impact on American culture? I contend that it is chiefly because the speech is a symbolic enactment of a redemption drama, in which ontological human guilt, and especially white America's guilt over racism, is symbolically purged. Some spoke of the speech as a "spiritual experience" (Hampton and Fayer, 1990, p. 168) or an "emotional catharsis" (Spillers, 1971, p. 22). D. H. Smith's (1964) remark that the speech "brought about a mass catharsis . . . the guilt of oppression and the yoke of subjugation were released in a torrent of passion and tears" (pp. 224–225), summarizes the point; but neither he, nor any other rhetorical critic, has developed that thesis to demonstrate how the speech achieves this effect.

Before fully developing that thesis it is necessary to briefly introduce Burke's concept of a "redemption drama" and explain how the term "redemption" is being used in this book. The process of guilt-purification-redemption is pivotal to Burke's theory of dramatism and symbolic action. It is a secular version of the Christian view of the soul's journey from hell to purgatory to heaven. For Burke, guilt-purification-redemption is a constantly repeating symbolic ritual that responds to an archetypal need in humans as symbol-using animals (Burke, 1970, pp. 4–5, 223; Foss, Foss and Trapp, 1985, pp. 178, 182; Rueckert, 1982, pp. 46–47, 128, 133). Rueckert (1982) notes that in Burke's theory of symbolic action:

> The three main archetypal clusters are pollution (hell), purification (purgatory), and redemption (heaven). The movement from the first to the last through purification constitutes the pattern of the rhetoric of rebirth and is the prime function of symbolic action. . . . no symbolic act is complete unless it contains images of all three clusters in the pattern. (p. 104)

That King would employ a rhetoric of redemption in his appeal to the nation is hardly surprising considering that he was a Christian preacher. In chapters 1 and 2 it was shown that the themes of redemption and reconciliation—embodied in the concept of the "beloved community"—were central to King's thinking. He often said that the goal of the civil rights movement was to "save the soul of America" (Downing, 1986, p. 4; Vivian, 1970, p. 98). By employing the term "redemption" in this study, I am using it in both its religious and secular senses. The word originally comes from the Latin verb *redimere*, meaning to buy back or repurchase something one formerly possessed. As the word has evolved over the centuries it has come to have both a religious and a secular meaning. In a religious or spiritual sense "redeem" means to deliver or save one's soul from the consequences of sin (as Christ did for humanity). In a secular sense "redeem" has been used in several senses, ranging from the act of freeing someone from a charge or claim to the act of atoning or making amends for past wrongs (*Oxford English Dictionary*, 1989, Vol. 13, p. 410). In King's thinking, as in black religion in general, "redemption" is often employed in a sense which contains both its religious and secular meanings simultaneously. This dual nature of redemption as both this-worldly and otherworldly is a chief tenet of black religion (Cone, 1984, pp. 213–214; Miller, 1992, pp. 35, 40). It is based on the argument that human beings have both a physical and spiritual nature. Since we are physical beings, we are eligible for this-worldly liberation from oppression, and since we are spiritual, we are eligible for otherworldly salvation (Miller, 1992, p. 74; also, see M. L. King, 1981, p. 18). King was the inheritor of a black religious tradition in which spiritual and secular redemption were seen as different sides of the same coin, and his thinking reflects this intermingling of the religious with the secular (Henry, 1987, pp. 328–329; Lischer, 1995, p. 56). For King, the secular is suffused within the spiritual order, so there is no contradiction or tension between religious redemption and secular redemption. He believed that the religious and the social realms were interdependent (Hanigan, 1974, p. 88). King's rhetoric reflects an often ambiguous and murky synthesis of the spiritual with the secular. This ambiguity, this sliding back and forth between the spiritual and secular realms, infuses the secular within the spiritual (see chapter 4) and gives King's rhetoric broad power and appeal, as exemplified in the "Dream" speech. Lucaites and Condit (1990) argue that the "Dream" speech merges Christianity with American secular mythology (pp. 15–17). But this melding also produces a weakness and limitation because it redefines political issues in spiritual terms. It allows King to elide social complexities through appeal to religious imagery and secular mythology.

By appealing to the need for national, secular redemption, King was invoking a very potent national myth. America's central myth is its conception of itself as a chosen people, a new nation with a God-given mission to redeem the world by providing a refuge of freedom, democracy, and opportunity (Jewett, 1973, p. 9; Merk, 1963, pp. 3–5, 261–266; Robertson, 1980, pp. 25–26, 122). Jewett and Lawrence (1988) argue that while the traditional "monomyth" of other cultures is based on rites of initiation and passage, the American "monomyth" is a secularized version of the Judeo-Christian redemption drama (p. xii). Duncan (1962) claims "the Christian drama of man's fall and redemption is the most powerful [social drama] produced thus far in our society" (p. 320). Williamson (2002) says the redemption drama "is an archetypal rhetorical form present in both the Old and New Testament, the narrative calculus of which has long been secularized" (p. 247). King's use of a redemption drama not only allowed him access to the powerful Christian symbolism of salvation, but also allowed him to merge that with the potent American mythology of secular redemption.

The need for redemption takes the form of a drama because any "principle of social order must be personified in some kind of dramatic action if it is to be comprehensible to all classes and conditions of man" (Duncan, 1968, p. 64). As Metz (1977) points out, Christian soteriology (the theology of redemption) does not function as interpretation and argumentation, but as narrative (pp. 332–333). Thus, King's representative anecdote (synecdochal narrative) in the "Dream" speech is a redemption drama in which a nation that has failed to live up to its promises is redeemed through the fulfillment of its creed. However, as we will see in the analysis, King elides the secular/religious distinction of redemption. That is, in King's discourse it is ambiguous whether that fulfillment is in the sociopolitical, this-worldly sense, or the spiritual-eschatological, otherwordly sense. King's rhetoric synthesizes the religious and secular senses of "redemption."

DRAMATIC ALIGNMENT

My analysis adopts Conrad's (1984) approach to the process of dramatistic criticism which involves three steps: (1) a statistical analysis of terms involving an inductive search for the dramatic alignment of the work; (2) the search for the representative anecdote; and (3) pentadic analysis. I have already identified the representative anecdote, and most of the remainder of this book explains how that anecdote functions in the rhetoric of King's address, but first it is necessary to explicate the other two steps in the process.

The search for the dramatic alignment of a work requires a cluster-agon analysis. Although Burke never summarizes this method in one place, it has been developed by others (see Berthold, 1976; Rueckert, 1982, pp. 83–111). To do a cluster analysis one selects the key term in the discourse being studied based on frequency and intensity of use. This is the speaker's ultimate "god-term." Then the critic looks for what term or terms go with that term, or cluster about it (Berthold, 1976, pp. 302–303; Rueckert, 1982, pp. 83–84). The ultimate god-term in King's "Dream" speech is "freedom." The word "freedom" appears twenty times, and the word "free" four times, in the speech. King opens the speech by stating that the purpose of the "act" (i.e., the March on Washington, and thereby the speech itself) is "freedom": "I am happy to join with you today in what will go down in history as the greatest demonstration *for freedom* in the history of our nation" [emphasis added] (M. L. King, 1963d, p. 723). In his closing sentence, King uses the word "freedom" twice and the word "free" three times. (In my later analysis of transcendence I will examine how King's use of the word "freedom" evolves throughout the speech, but for now I only want to indicate the basic dramatic alignment of the work.) The main term that King clusters with "freedom" is "justice," which he uses seven times, as when he speaks of "the riches of freedom and the security of justice" (M. L. King, 1963d, p. 724). The terms "freedom" and/or "justice" are also clustered with the terms "rights," "equality," and "democracy."

To discern the forces of opposition the critic must perform an agon analysis to go along with the cluster analysis (Berthold, 1976, p. 303). Burke says that in searching for dramatic alignment, we should look for "What is vs. what." A drama, or agon, will contain the "principles," a "protagonist" and "antagonist," and the "satellites" or "adjuncts" associated with the principles (Burke, 1973, pp. 69, 76). The cluster analysis revealed that King's ultimate god-term is "freedom." Thus, the protagonist in King's drama is "freedom" and its satellite terms are "justice," "equality," "democracy," and "rights." While there is not one overall devil-term that King uses extensively as the antagonist, "freedom" and "justice" are obviously in conflict with the cluster of antagonistic terms "injustice" (used three times), "segregation" (used twice), "discrimination" (used once), and "vicious racists" (used once). Thus, the protagonists, the god-terms of "freedom" and "justice," are in conflict with the antagonists, the devil-terms of "injustice," "discrimination," and "racism," for the soul of America. (The cluster-agon analysis is taken up at greater length in chapter 4 where it is used to demonstrate King's methods of purification through transcendence and dramatic catharsis.)

PENTADIC RATIO ANALYSIS

In pentadic ratio analysis the critic goes beyond identifying the parts of the pentad in the discourse under study, to identifying interrelationships between pentadic terms to demonstrate how an element or attribute of one term is "implicitly or analogically" present in another (Burke, 1968b, p. 446). For example, if a rhetor employs a "scene-act ratio" then he or she is positing that a certain scene implies or calls for a certain act in response (Burke, 1969a, p. 3). Following the Burkean practice of conceiving of ratios in pairs (scene-act, scene-agent, act-purpose, act-agent, etc.; see Burke, 1969a, p. 15) we could say that in the "I Have a Dream" speech King employs a scene-act ratio in which the scene (described in the first half of the speech as an America that has failed to provide racial justice) implies the need for a certain act (national redemption). However, redemption is really a purpose that requires or implies that an act of purification has taken place. Thus, in this case conceiving of the ratio as a triad better fits the discourse under study, and corresponds to the three elements of the redemption drama. Guilt, purification, and redemption all imply one another. Guilt implies the need for redemption, which takes place through some process of purification. So in this case the pentadic ratio is a triad in which the scene of an America blighted by racial injustice (guilt) calls for an act of purification for the purpose of redemption. Thus, we have a triadic pentadic ratio that corresponds to the representative anecdote (synecdochal narrative) of this speech:

Pentadic Ratio	scene	act	purpose
Narrative Form	guilt	purification	redemption

This schematic representation of the structure of the speech will be expanded upon and added to in later chapters in order to integrate the analyses provided in chapters 4 and 5.

To be an effective rhetorical pattern the logic of this particular scene-act-purpose relationship must be shared by the audience. I maintain that the guilt-purification-redemption model is an intersubjective social/cultural form that was common property in the Judeo-Christian America of 1963. It is, in other words, a "constitutive practice." Extending Searle's notion of "constitutive rules"—rules inseparable from the behavior they govern—Taylor (1985) argues that there are also constitutive "practices" which are inseparable from the language we use to describe them (pp. 34–35). Thus, a concept, that is, guilt, must be embedded in a larger structure of language and culture by which we agree upon what one should feel guilty about and how one should react to a sense of guilt (see Taylor, 1985, pp. 23–24). Therefore, in a Judeo-Christian culture, if there is guilt (sin), there is a need for redemption, and to achieve redemption, there must be some process of purification (see Burke, 1970, pp. 4–5; and Williamson, 2002, p. 247). Thus, in the context of the civil rights movement, one must consider the range of meanings available to a rhetor in a Judeo-Christian culture such as the America of 1963. If racism is immoral (sinful), then there is by the logic of the cultural practice—the "constitutive" practice—a need to make up for (redeem) that sin; and if there is a need for redemption, then there is a need for some process of purification or cleansing of that sin and its accompanying guilt. Thus, in Burke's terms, King employs a "scene-act-purpose ratio" in which the scene—an America blighted by the sin of racial injustice—calls for a particular act—the purification of that guilt—in order to achieve a certain purpose—racial reconciliation and the social redemption of the nation. As was argued above, the myth of America's redemptive role in history is the central American myth. King's speech had such immediate impact and long-term appeal because he effectively exploits this basic (and implicit) cultural attitude. As Reik (1957) has noted, "the guilt feeling of a group, of a nation, or of all nations need not be conscious to unfold tremendous effects" (pp. 40–41).

BURKE'S THEORY OF GUILT

In Burke's theory, guilt is ontological, due to humans' symbol-using nature. Human symbol-using capacity results in the creation of hierarchy, the idea of the negative, and the concept of perfection, all of which lead to guilt. According to Burke, language inevitably leads to the development of some type of social order, that is, hierarchy. In a differentiated social structure, guilt about one's place in the structure will arise. Those higher up in the hierarchy will feel guilty about their privilege, while those lower down will feel guilty that they have not risen higher.[1] Language also allows humans to create the concept of the negative, the idea that there are certain things one should not do. Any social order will thus create hundreds of "thou-shalt-nots." But no one is capable of upholding all of the rules of the social order, and in some way will fail or disobey. Failure and disobedience—the "fall of man" in the archetypal religious motif—results in guilt.[2] And finally, according to Burke, symbol use contains within itself an inevitable perfectionistic tendency, in which the symbol-users strive toward the creation of terms designating ultimate states of perfection. But since humans will inevitably fall short of their notions of perfection, guilt ensues.[3]

The fact that humans feel guilt initiates the guilt-purification-redemption cycle. Guilt creates the need for redemption, and purification is any means through which redemption is achieved. Since guilt is inherent in human nature, redemption is never permanent. Thus, there is a never-ending need in humans for symbolic purification and the ritual of rebirth is an ever-repeating cycle (Burke, 1970, pp. 223, 231). Although the concept of "guilt" is crucial in Burke's theory, he never actually defines the term. However, we can get a good sense of what he means by "guilt" from the way he uses the term—that is, by seeing what terms he clusters with guilt and uses as synonyms for guilt—and by what he speaks of as requiring redemption. While Burke's concept of guilt contains the usual meaning of the term as a sense of responsibility or shame for having done wrong, he extends the parameters of the concept. For Burke, guilt is a sort of ontological human sense of anxiety, a feeling of separation from others, or the failure to live up to standards imposed by self and society. Burke speaks of guilt in terms of "anxiety" (1970, p. 236); "sin" (1966, pp. 15, 144; 1970, pp. 112, 176, 181, 222, 228); "disobedience" (1970, pp. 176, 242); "differentiation" (1966, p. 15; 1970, p. 202); and "disorder" (1970, pp. 190, 242). Foss, Foss, and Trapp (1985) state that in Burke's system other words for guilt are "anxiety," "social tension," and "embarrassment" (p. 178). Duncan (1962) describes Burke's concept of guilt as a situation of "profound social disrelationship" that "arises out of *negation* of the principles of social order" [emphasis in original]; or, in other words, it is the "sin of disobedience" to the social order (p. 121).

In sum, Burke's theory is that guilt ontologically arises out of humans' nature as symbol-using animals, and thus there is need for expiation of our guilt to achieve a state of guiltlessness (redemption), which is nonetheless temporary. The idea that guilt is an inherent aspect of human nature that requires rituals of purification is not unique to Burke. The notion that guilt is ontological, or at least that it is a significant factor in human motivation, is shared by many other scholars. Reik (1957) argues that guilt feeling is common to humankind and that a universal sense of guilt or a similar idea appears in the works of Schopenhauer, Nietzsche, Kierkegaard, Heidegger, Shakespeare, Dostoyevsky, Tolstoy, Sartre, Faulkner, and others, and in theological terms, as sin, in religions from ancient times to today (pp. 41–43). Carroll (1985) argues that guilt is "the essence of humaneness," and that it is through sublimation of guilt that people create a culture. Therefore, he maintains, it is necessary for a culture to provide means for individuals to "sublimate" their guilt in socially constructive ways (pp. 1, 139–167). Buber (1965) urges psychotherapists to understand the "ontic character" of guilt, "whose place is not the soul but being" (p. 123). The confession of guilt in a public and socially prescribed manner can lead to a type of "reconciliation," which Buber terms "illumination" (p. 137). The need to expiate guilt is not unique to Western Judeo-Christian culture. In *The Golden Bough*, Frazer (1911–1915) cites numerous examples of rites of purification and expiation across many different cultures. Perera (1986) writes that the scapegoat phenomenon, a common mode of purification, is almost universal (p. 9), and that the various "atonement and riddance-of-evil ceremonies" found in many cultures are attempts "to excise the evils that afflict mankind, whether these be death, disease, violence . . . or the sense of sin and guilt that accompanies knowledge of transgressions of the moral code" (p. 11).

Burke is the only theorist I am aware of who finds the source of guilt in language, but Buber's analysis of why humans feel guilt is instructive. Buber (1965) argues that to understand the human "capacity and tendency" for guilt, one must bear in mind that man is the only creature that separates himself not only from his environment, but also from himself—he thus becomes a "detached object" about which he can reflect and condemn (p. 134). Buber leaves it at that, but a Burkean would argue that Buber fails to recognize that humans have this capacity to separate themselves from themselves—to objectify themselves—because they have the capacity for language. It is only because we have the capacity to speak of the self linguistically (objectify the self), and measure that self against linguistic constructs known as rules or norms of behavior, that we can feel a sense of failure. It is only because our language allows us to create a hierarchy of values, and to establish ethical norms, that humans can function in a moral-ethical realm. Without the objectifying, moralizing capacity of language humans could not feel guilt, for there would be nothing about which to feel guilty. It is only through language that an "I" can feel anxiety and division—whether from separation from another (a "you" or a "them"), or from disobedience (sin) to the linguistically constructed norms of the social order. Buber (1965) writes that man is capable of guilt because he has a "conscience" which allows him to distinguish between those "actions which should be approved and those which should be disapproved" (p. 134). But, Burke would say that man has a conscience because he has language. Language allows such concepts as "actions which should be approved" and "actions which should be disapproved," and it is that distinction which creates the "conscience."

KING'S USE OF GUILT

Other scholars have noted that King's rhetorical strategy involved evoking a sense of guilt in white Americans (Lewis, 1978, p. 394; Lischer, 1995, p. 155; D. H. Smith, 1964, pp. 145, 182); and Payne (1989) makes this point with respect to the "I Have a Dream" speech specifically (p. 50). Meier's (1965) analysis of the source of King's rhetorical effectiveness is especially insightful in this regard. Since he sums up well King's use of the guilt-purification-redemption pattern, I will quote him at length.

> [King] unerringly knows how to exploit to maximum effectiveness their [whites'] growing feeling of guilt. . . . With intuitive, but extraordinary skill, he not only castigates whites for their sins but, in contrast to angry young writers like [James] Baldwin, he explicitly states his belief in their salvation. Not only will direct action bring fulfillment of the "American Dream" to Negroes but the Negroes' use of direct action will help whites to live up to their Christian and democratic values; it will purify, cleanse and heal the sickness in white society. Whites will benefit as well as Negroes. He has faith that the white man will re-

> deem himself. . . . King arouses the guilt feelings of whites, and then relieves them. . . . King's performance provides an extraordinary catharsis for the white listener. (p. 54)

King himself was very much aware that his strategy involved evoking a sense of guilt in white Americans. Just a few months before the March on Washington, in an interview with Kenneth Clark, King said that the nonviolent movement "arouses a sense of shame within them [the white community]. . . . I think it does something to touch the conscience and establish a sense of guilt" (Clark, 1963, p. 42; also, see M. L. King, 1981, p. 121).

King's notion of white guilt was quite Burkean. For King, whites felt guilt over segregation because they knew in their hearts that segregation was wrong (see M. L. King, 1986, pp. 357–358). He spoke of segregation as a "glaring evil" which "is a blatant denial of the unity which we have in Christ" (M. L. King, 1957a, p. 32; 1958, p. 205). Segregation was a sin, a moral failure of the nation to live up to certain principles of its social order, which thus created a kind of division, which King often called schizophrenia. In *Stride toward Freedom*, he wrote:

> America has manifested a schizophrenic personality on the question of race. She has been torn between selves—a self in which she has proudly professed democracy and a self in which she has sadly practiced the antithesis of democracy. . . . This contradiction has disturbed the conscience of whites both North and South. (M. L. King, 1958, pp. 190–191)

In his "Letter from Birmingham City Jail," King called segregation "morally wrong and sinful" and then presented an almost Burkean analysis of the ontological nature of sin as manifested in segregation: "Paul Tillich has said that sin is separation. Isn't segregation an existential expression of man's tragic separation, an expression of his awful estrangement, his terrible sinfulness?" (M. L. King, 1986, pp. 293–294).

GUILT IN "I HAVE A DREAM"

The ritual of rebirth in King's speech is as much collective as individual; that is, the guilt, and thus the need for redemption, is national and the individual partakes of the guilt-purification-redemption process through membership in the collectivity. The idea of guilt and redemption as collective goes back at least to the Hebrew Old Testament. According to Reik (1957), the concept of collective guilt, of a social group or community sharing in a sense of guilt or responsibility, is found in ancient civilizations (pp. 34–36). Burke (1970) has noted that guilt, and thus the need for redemption, can be extended to "the idea of nationality" (p. 232). The notion of collective guilt is possible because, just as individuals have a conscience, nations have a collective conscience. Just as individuals have an "identity" which they can measure against norms of individual behavior, nations have a "national identity," which they can measure against standards of national behavior. Thus, a nation can feel guilt for not living up to its principles.

When seeking to absolve guilt the "first step is the symbolization of our guilt in some form which makes possible confrontation of our guilt" (Duncan, 1968, p. 138). In August of 1963, with the images of Birmingham still fresh in the national consciousness, King had a reservoir of symbolizations of guilt to tap into. King's verbal depictions of America's racial injustice against blacks resonated with a panoply of images that had entered the national consciousness in the years and months leading up to the March on Washington—the Little Rock and Ole Miss desegregation crises, the violence against the Freedom Riders, Bull Connor's brutality in Birmingham, George Wallace's stand in the schoolhouse door, the murder of Emmett Till and the assassination of Medgar Evers in Mississippi—revealing the great distance between America's principles and its practices.

In King's speech America's guilt is symbolized through all three of Burke's sources of guilt: hierarchy, the negative, and the principle of perfection. Hierarchy is manifested in the sociopolitical structure of America in which

> the Negro is still sadly crippled by the manacles of segregation and the chains of discrimination . . . lives on a lonely island of poverty in the midst of a vast ocean of material prosperity . . . [and] is still languished in the corners of American society and finds himself an exile in his own land. (M. L. King, 1963d, p. 723)

King then adds: "So we've come here today to dramatize a *shameful* condition" [emphasis added] (M. L. King, 1963d, p. 723).

Guilt is also revealed in the combination of the principle of perfection and the negative, that is, the failure of the nation to achieve its ideals of justice and equality. According to Burke (1970), humans strive toward their perception of perfection (p. 296). To explain his concept of perfection Burke (1966) uses the Aristotelian concept of "'entelechy,' the notion that each being aims at the perfection natural to its kind" (p. 17; see also Lindsay, 1998). Humans express their concepts of perfection, of course, in symbols (Burke, 1970, p. 297), what Burke (1970) calls the "search for the title of titles," a "secular summarizing term," or a "god-term" (p. 25). The entelechal principle for the society or collectivity is summed up in King's use of the god-term "justice," which he uses seven times. "Justice" is indeed a term of perfection. It is a word created by the symbol-users to represent their concept of perfect equity and equality (or nonhierarchy) that would be the *telos* or entelechal purpose of their concept of "society." What the god-term "justice" is for society, the god-term "freedom" represents for the individual (Burke, 1970, pp. 281–283), that is "the perfection natural to its kind." As noted earlier, King uses the word "freedom" or "free" twenty-four times in the "Dream" speech. Like the word "justice," "freedom" is a term expressing an idea of perfection, only attainable symbolically and only able to be conceived at all because of the symbol-using nature of the species.

By combining the negative with these terms of perfection, these god-terms (and the terms they cluster with), we get failure to live up to our concepts of perfection at the societal and individual levels—failure to live up to our national principles—thus guilt. King uses the term "injustice" (i.e., the negative plus justice) three times, and the phrase "not free" once. But also, of course, the god-terms are used within the context of the negative. Hence, we hear that America has "*defaulted* on this promissory note" to provide "the unalienable rights of life, liberty, and the pursuit of happiness" and that "America has given the Negro people a *bad* check, a check which has come back marked '*insufficient* funds'" [all emphases added] (M. L. King, 1963d, p. 724).

In Burke's theory guilt is inherent in human symbol-using activity. The guilt exists before the rhetor speaks. The rhetor's challenge is not to convince the audience of its guilt, but to symbolically manifest their preexistent guilt in a manner consistent with the sources of that guilt so it can be absolved through purification. In the situation in which King was speaking, there was not the time, or even the need, to present a thorough exposition of the necessity for and sources of white guilt. King's brief references to conditions under which blacks lived and the failure of America to live up to its principles "insofar as her citizens of color are concerned," evoked images and symbolizations already present in the nation's consciousness.

NOTES

1. On hierarchy as inevitable in the nature of language, see Burke (1969b, pp. 141, 279). On hierarchy as leading to guilt, see Burke (1966, pp. 15, 144; 1970, pp. 4–5).

2. On the negative as the result of symbol use, see Burke (1966, pp. 9, 419–420, 469; 1970, pp. 18, 283). On a sense of guilt arising from the negative, see Burke (1970, pp. 285, 294) and Rueckert (1982, p. 131).

3. On the principle of perfection as contained in symbolicity, see Burke (1966, pp. 16–17; 1970, p. 296). On the principle of perfection creating guilt, see Burke (1966, pp. 18–20; 1970, pp. 297–300).

4

Purification and Redemption

Purification is the fulcrum of the process of guilt-purification-redemption. In "I Have a Dream" King effects purification through symbolic victimage and mortification, rhetorical transcendence, and images of change, movement, and dramatic catharsis. Redemption is the temporary condition that follows upon purification of guilt.

Any means whereby guilt is absolved is purification. In Burke's theory guilt is inherent in human nature, and redemption is the result of the process of purification, so the key question to ask in applying the guilt-purification-redemption theory is: How does the rhetor take the listener from guilt to redemption, that is, how does he or she achieve symbolic purification for the audience? Since achieving symbolic purification of guilt is the major rhetorical challenge in the rhetoric of redemption, most of this chapter deals with the means through which King achieves symbolic purification for his audience. There are many ways in which a rhetor may accomplish symbolic purification for an audience and the multiplicity of ways in which King achieves rhetorical purification increases the effectiveness of his speech.

In considering King's use of the religiously oriented concept of purification and redemption, we should not lose sight of the secular function of this type of rhetoric. Social authorities not only define what constitutes a transgression of the social order, they must also provide means of expiating or absolving the guilt people feel for violating the social order (Duncan, 1962, pp. 125, 285; 1968, pp. 75, 140). By providing means of expiating white and black guilt (black guilt will be discussed in the next section) King hoped to create an environment in which racial reconciliation could take place. Thus King's redemption drama serves as more than a means of providing symbolic spiritual purification of guilt. He also is assigning his auditors roles in a civic polity and building a sense of identification through connecting whites and blacks to a heritage of democratic ideals. The spiritual element allows King to place civic reconciliation within the context of the divine order (see the section on transcendence in this chapter). The religious and secular mythology gives King discursive forms for justifying and making sense of his civic and legislative goals. That is not to imply that King did not genuinely want to improve his listeners' "souls" as well. The point here is that King, or another rhetor in this same situation, could have made other rhetorical choices. He could have sought to indict American racial injustice without providing hope of redemption. He could have dealt with the issue in purely secular terms without the religious context. For example, he could have chosen to constitute his auditors as citizens of the world in a secular sense and America as a member of the world community of nations. He could have rejected the American dream as materialistic, or as a sham. Although these are not likely choices for King—given what we know about his thinking and what he had said in the past (see chapter 2), and given the church-based nature of the civil rights movement—the rhetoric of this speech reflects choices that King and the movement made at some point about how to appeal to the nation for racial justice. King chose to justify the movement in terms of America's image of itself as a just nation, thereby constituting the civil rights movement as an epic battle or a great test in that nation's struggle to perfect democracy, and placing that struggle within the context of morality and justice in God's divine order. He expertly exploited the human tendency toward symbolizations of its ideals of perfection (Williamson, 2002, p. 246). These rhetorical choices had certain consequences for the civil rights movement at the time, and for shaping subsequent public discourse on civil rights and race relations in general. Those consequences will be considered in chapter 7, but for now I will examine how purification of guilt functions in King's speech.

VICTIMAGE AND MORTIFICATION

Burke (1966) defines victimage as "purification by sacrifice, by *vicarious atonement*, unburdening of guilt within by transference to chosen vessels without" [emphasis in original] (p. 478). Thus, victimage is transference of guilt to a "scapegoat" (see Burke, 1966, p. 435; 1969a, p. 406; 1973, pp. 39–40, 202–203). While victimage absolves guilt "homicidally," in the slaying of the scapegoat, mortification absolves guilt "suicidally," in self-punishment and self-denial (Burke, 1970, pp. 190, 223; 1973, p. 435; Rueckert, 1982, p. 146). These two modes of purification are closely related, because while victimage is the mortification of the other (the scapegoat), mortification is the victimizing or scapegoating of the self (Burke, 1970, p. 248; Rueckert, 1982, pp. 146–150; Scheibel, 2002, pp. 310–313). In King's "I Have a Dream" speech, the attempt is made to absolve black guilt through a type of mortification, or victimage of the self. Even though black suffering is not self-inflicted, as mortification implies, it is nonetheless purificatory to see oneself as a victim or scapegoat for others. Although we normally do not think of African Americans as having anything about which to feel "guilty" in regard to the history of race relations in America, in a Burkean sense black people do feel guilt and anxiety. In Burke's theory guilt is inherent in human nature. Just as those "Up" in the hierarchy are guilty of not being "Down," those "Down" are guilty of not being "Up" (Burke, 1966, p. 15). Therefore, black guilt differs from white guilt in that black guilt grows out of African Americans' historical status as an oppressed minority. An oppressed minority will often feel guilt and shame because it comes to accept the negative image of itself held up to it by the dominant majority. This can result in a sense of inferiority and self-hate (Downing, 1986, p. 189). Dyson (2000) claims that "Black guilt" resulted from a failure to demand dignity and respect (p. 36). Steele (1990) argues that just as "guilt is the essence of white anxiety . . . inferiority is the essence of black anxiety" (p. 144). Martin Luther King (1958) felt that segregation had caused African Americans to feel "a tragic sense of inferiority" (p. 190; also, see M. L. King, 1957b; 1981, p. 110).

The cleansing of guilt must be contrived in a manner consistent with the source of that guilt (Burke, 1966, pp. 351–352). Thus, King's rhetoric cleanses black guilt by transforming the very conditions of that guilt, oppression and socioeconomic inferiority, into a virtue. King purifies black guilt and anxiety because his vivid depictions of black suffering at the hands of white society calls on associations which cast blacks as martyrs for a greater good. Burke (1970) says that martyrdom "is the fulfillment of the principle of mortification . . . with the self as scapegoat" (p. 248). Burke (1970) also notes "mortification is the exercising of oneself in 'virtue'" (p. 190). In King's rhetoric, African Americans become virtuous martyrs who have suffered in order to redeem America of its sins and to force the nation to live up to its ideals. While King does not use the literal phrase "virtuous martyr" in his speeches or writings, the idea that blacks should turn their suffering into a virtue and teach nonviolence and love to America and the world, permeates King's speeches and writings (see M. L. King, 1957a, pp. 29–30; 1958, pp. 214–216, 220; 1964b, p. 14; 1981, pp. 54–55, 121; 1986, pp. 10–11, 41–42). For example, King (1958) wrote that "the Negro" may be God's instrument for injecting "a new spiritual dynamic" into Western civilization (p. 224). He told black church audiences that "Our present suffering and our nonviolent struggle to be free may well offer to Western civilization the kind of spiritual dynamic so desperately needed for survival" (M. L. King, 1981, p. 92).

In purifying African Americans through symbolizing their status as virtuous martyrs, King was drawing upon a strong tradition in black religious and intellectual thought which held that the history of suffering and oppression endured by African Americans had made them morally superior to their oppressors and given them a messiah-like mission to redeem their oppressors (see Fullinwider, 1969). The notion that the oppressed are morally superior to their oppressors is common in human thought, and oppressed groups often compensate for low material and social status by seeing themselves as superior in moral virtue (Robertson, 1980, p. 104; Russell, 1950). Baldwin (1991) argued that "King considered black people generally more humane than their white oppressors" because white America's obsession with racism and wealth, and its historic quest for power over other people, had resulted in a loss of spirituality and higher human values (p. 237). King (1981) said that America's scientific and material progress had "outdistanced" its moral and spiritual progress (pp. 73–74, 139). King himself does not explicitly say that blacks are morally superior to whites, but the idea is implied in his notion that the African American experience of suffering and oppression gives blacks a mission to redeem white America from its sins (see Baldwin, 1991, pp. 231–243; Cone, 1986, p. 26). For example, in his statement to the press before his trip to be awarded the Nobel Peace Prize, King (1964a) said:

> Peace in this nation and in the world is due in large measure to the willingness of Negro Americans to suffer injustice and persecution and their ability to respond to their oppressors with Love. This may be the most significant fact in the world today—that God has entrusted his black children in America to teach the world to love, and to live together in brotherhood. (p. 1)

This "mission ideology"—the idea that through their Christlike suffering God would use African Americans to save humankind and bring about the kingdom of God on earth—developed early in black religious thought, was accepted by twentieth-century black intellectuals, and became a cornerstone of King's philosophy. Robertson (1980) argues that African Americans came to see themselves as America's Jews, a Chosen People, who, Christlike in their suffering, wisdom, and morality, were sent to America to redeem the nation and make it truly free "by bringing its great promise of equality to fruition" (p. 105). Fullinwider (1969) traces the evolution of this myth from post–Civil War black preachers through twentieth-century black intellectuals such as W. E. B. DuBois, Charles S. Johnson, and James Baldwin. Fullinwider maintains that King adopted the Christlike mythology and mission ideology of the black race from the milieu of his home-life as the son of a Baptist minister and in the halls of Morehouse College, which is one of the places where the doctrine was being preached in the 1940s when King did his undergraduate work there (pp. 231–232). According to Walton (1971), the "concept of the black's 'saving' mission in America" was "central to King's political thought" (p. 7). "In [King's] view, blacks had a mission to fulfill beyond their struggle for justice and equality, namely, the introduction of a new moral standard in American life" (Walton, 1971, p. 31). According to Baldwin (1991), "King espoused this concept [of the black messianic mission] so consistently that it should be accounted a fundamental component of his thought" (p. 230). King's own words often reflected his belief in the black mission. In his first speech of the Montgomery bus boycott on December 5, 1955, King stated:

> [W]hen the history books are written in the future, somebody will have to say, "There lived a race of people, a *black* people, 'fleecy locks and black complexion,' a people who had the moral courage to stand up for their rights. And thereby they injected a new meaning into the veins of history and of civilization." And we're gonna do that. God grant that we will do it before it is too late. (emphasis in original) (Carson, 1997, p. 74)

In *Stride toward Freedom* King wrote that he prayed that "the Negro" would recognize the "necessity of suffering" and "make of it a virtue." He implored "the Negro . . . to see the ordeals of this generation as the opportunity to transfigure himself and American society" (M. L. King, 1958, p. 220). A recurrent theme in King's speeches and writings was that "unearned suffering is redemptive" (Ansbro, 1982, p. 7; M. L. King, 1958, pp. 103, 179; 1963d, p. 725; Oates, 1982, p. 79).

Thus, in depicting black suffering and victimage in his "Dream" speech, King was drawing upon a classic African American and Christian theme, that suffering is expiatory and makes one virtuous. King purifies blacks of guilt by making them martyrs at the altar of American ideals of freedom and justice, when he describes "Negro slaves" as having been "seared in the flames of withering injustice;" and blacks as "crippled by the manacles of segregation and the chains of discrimination," and "languished in the corners of American society" (M. L. King, 1963d, p. 723). *Thus, we see that the very images that symbolize guilt for white America purify guilt for black America*. The process of purification through black victimage and martyrdom can also be discerned in the following words that describe African Americans as:

> [V]ictim[s] of the unspeakable horrors of police brutality. . . [whose] bodies, heavy with the fatigue of travel, cannot gain lodging in the motels of the highways and the hotels of the cities . . . [and whose] children are stripped of their selfhood and robbed of their dignity by signs stating "For Whites Only." (M. L. King, 1963d, p. 725)

Solomon (1980) writes that a group's perception of itself as a moral agent is expiatory (p. 59); and I earlier noted Burke's (1970) claim that exercising oneself in "virtue" is a type of mortification (p. 190). The "perfect" victim is one who has been made worthy by reason of his or her virtue (as was Christ), one who is "too good for this world" (Burke, 1970, pp. 242, 252; 1973, p. 40). Purification through virtue is symbolized when King tells his people not to resort to violence in gaining their rights:

> In the process of gaining our rightful place we must not be guilty of wrongful deeds. . . . We must forever conduct our struggle on the high plane of dignity and discipline. We must not allow our creative protest to degenerate into physical violence. Again and again we must rise to the majestic heights of meeting physical force with soul force. (M. L. King, 1963d, p. 724)

In the following section King combines martyrdom with virtue, and explicitly promises his followers that their suffering will redeem them:

> I am not mi- [sic] unmindful that some of you have come here out of *great trials and tribulations*. Some of you have come fresh from narrow jail cells. Some of you have come from areas where your crest- [sic] quest for freedom left you battered by the *storms of persecution* and staggered by the winds of police brutality. You have been the veterans of *creative suffering*. Continue to work with the faith that *unearned suffering is redemptive.* [emphases mine] (M. L. King, 1963d, p. 725)

In short, King's rhetoric tells African Americans that their suffering and virtue have purified their guilt and made them worthy of redemption.

TRANSCENDENCE

While King absolves black guilt through images of black victimage and virtue, white guilt, as well as black guilt, is absolved through transcendence. Transcendence is a means of purification that has largely been ignored by Burkean scholars (an exception is Brummett, 1981; 1982) in favor of an almost exclusive focus on victimage and mortification. While Burke speaks most often of purification taking place through victimage or mortification (see, for example, Burke, 1966, pp. 435, 478; 1970, pp. 190, 223, 248), he does mention transcendence as a means of purification. For example, Burke (1973) writes that "criminality" (or guilt) can be "*transformed, transcended, transubstantiated*, by incorporation into a wider context of symbolic action" [emphasis in original] (p. 52), and he claims that abstraction, transcendence, and ultimate hierarchy are among the many "modes of symbolic purification ingrained in the nature of symbolic action" (cited in Rueckert, 1982, p. 137; see also, Burke, 1984a, p. 73). It is fairly obvious why humans regard victimage and mortification as expiatory of guilt. Victimage places the guilt upon another (the scapegoat), who is then sacrificed for the good of the community. Mortification rids one of guilt because one has thus suffered for (paid for) one's sins (see Burke, 1970, p. 176). But, what is transcendence, and how does it expiate guilt?

In Burke's theory transcendence is basic to language and thought. It takes place every time we name something, for in assigning a symbol to a thing, we are, to a degree, transcending the thing symbolized by translating the non-symbolic into the symbolic (Burke, 1969b, pp. 192, 279; 1970, pp. 16, 21–22). Burke (1966) defines transcendence as "the building of a *terministic* bridge whereby one realm is *transcended* by being viewed in *terms* of a realm 'beyond' it" [all emphases in original] (p. 187). In other words, transcendence is "when one redefines some action as part of a new higher context" (Brummett, 1982, p. 549). Crucial to transcendence then, is the concept of hierarchy, for transcendence is essentially the act of moving up a hierarchy in which an action taking place in a lower realm of the hierarchy is *integrated into*, or put within the context of, a higher realm (see Burke, 1969b, pp. 187–189). As Duncan (1962) notes: "All hierarchy rests on progression from a lower to a higher stage. Thus any improvement of status is a kind of transcendence" (p. 323). It is important to emphasize, however, that one does not achieve rhetorical transcendence to a higher realm by completely rejecting the lower realm, but by *encompassing* the lower realm within the context of the higher realm. For examples of this we could look at the rhetoric of Abraham Lincoln, who used transcendence often. In his Gettysburg Address the physical realm is transcended for the political realm when Lincoln places the death of the soldiers at Gettysburg within the context of the greater purpose of keeping alive the democratic system. (This is a common technique of "war rhetoric" in which soldiers are portrayed as sacrificing their lives for a greater political good, "democracy," "freedom," etc.) In his Second Inaugural Address Lincoln transcends the physical and sociopolitical orders for the spiritual order when he speculates that the strife and bloodshed of the Civil War may be God's judgment upon the nation for the sin of slavery (for the Lincoln speeches, see Heffner, 1985, pp. 157, 161–163).

Why and how, then, can transcendence bring about purification of guilt? The idea is not unique to Burke, or even to Western thought. In Zen Buddhism one achieves Satori or nirvana—a state of enlightenment—by transcending the conscious realm; that is by integrating the conscious with the unconscious. Singh and Sirisena (1988) write: "The object of meditation is to integrate the part with the whole, the conscious mind with unconscious mind, and in this process of unification and transfiguration *Satori* is experienced" (p. 136). A similar concept is Jung's (1960) notion of the "transcendent function," in which one attains "liberation" by joining the conscious with the unconscious mind. Koestler (1978) argues that human beings have both "self-assertive" (or individualistic) needs and "self-transcending" or "integrative" needs. The latter arise out of the "need to belong, to transcend the narrow boundaries of the self and be part of a more embracing whole" (p. 60). Transcendence, then, eliminates division (guilt) by appeal to a higher principle under which various parts can be united. Since a social hierarchy will always contain differences, to absolve guilt over division and differentiation social authorities must be able to appeal to some higher principle that unites individuals, justifies social distinctions, and integrates the parts into a whole (see Duncan, 1962, pp. 279, 308; 1968, pp. 66, 130).

It could be argued that all modes of purification involve transcendence of some type. Perera (1986) notes that the scapegoat ritual originally had ties to the spiritual realm. The scapegoat was a human or animal victim chosen for sacrifice to propitiate a "god's anger and heal the community." Its purpose was to "bring the transpersonal dimension" to the aid and renewal of the community (p. 8). Mortification is a type of transcendence in which the physical/material realm is transcended for the spiritual/moral realm. Payne (1989) makes this point when he writes that King's recounting in the "Dream" speech of the horrors of slavery and the black struggle in America consoles blacks for their suffering by elevating spiritual values above material losses (pp. 49–50). Purification through change, movement, and dramatic catharsis—which will be examined later in this chapter—always involves transformation of some type in which an initial state of being is, in a sense, *transcended* by a new state of being.

BURKEAN TRANSCENDENCE IN "I HAVE A DREAM"

If purification, and thus redemption, can be achieved through transcendence, then how in Burke's theory does one achieve transcendence?

> Transcendence . . . is best got by processes of dialectic. . . . In dialectical transcendence, the principle of transformation operates in terms of a "beyond." It . . . "builds a bridge" between disparate realms. And insofar as things here and now are treated in terms of a "beyond," they thereby become infused or inspirited by the addition of a *new or further dimension.* [emphasis in original] (Burke, 1966, pp. 188–190)

In order to discern transcendence in a piece of discourse and evaluate how it operates, then, we must look for the terms that build bridges to new or higher dimensions. Burke (1970) describes the process as follows:

> First, there is the "Upward Way" from "lower terms" to a unitary transcendent term conceived "mythically" (analogically); and then there is a reversal of direction, a "Downward Way," back to "lower" terms with which the dialectician began his climb; but now the "lower" terms are viewed as having become modified by the unitary principle encountered en route. The secular, empirical terms are "infused by the spirit" of the transcendent term. (p. 37)

Burke's "cluster analysis" provides the critical method for discovering the way a rhetor achieves a dialectical transcendence, or movement upward. As the reader will recall from the explanation of the cluster-agon method in chapter 3, a cluster analysis involves a search for the speaker's key terms based on frequency and intensity of use. The critic then identifies the speaker's ultimate "god-term" to which the other terms are related in a subordinate manner. In other words, the critic looks for "what goes with what" (Burke, 1973, p. 22; see also, Berthold, 1976, p. 303). For example, Berthold's (1976) cluster analysis of John F. Kennedy's rhetoric concluded that Kennedy's god-term is "freedom," which he frequently links to four other key terms: "peace," "strength," "unity," and "defense" (pp. 304–306). As noted in chapter 3, the ultimate god-term in King's "Dream" speech is also "freedom." In his first sentence King describes the demonstration as being "for freedom," and he uses the term "freedom" twenty times and the term "free" four times throughout the speech. However, King uses "freedom" differently and clusters it with different terms than does Kennedy. Also, while King uses the term "freedom" throughout the speech, he is not always using it in the same sense. In other words, he takes it "up the hierarchy," using the term "freedom" to build a "terministic bridge" from the sociopolitical to the supernatural realm. Before employing cluster analysis to demonstrate how King achieves rhetorical transcendence, it is necessary to explain Burke's hierarchy of the realms to which words may refer.

Burke claims that there are four realms to which a word may refer. The first is the natural realm, which is that of material entities, biological classifications, physiological conditions, and the like. These are words such as "dog," "tree," "hunger," etc. Burke calls these "positive" terms. The second realm is that of "dialectical" terms. This is the sociopolitical realm dealing with social relations, laws, right and wrong, etc., and includes terms such as "good," "bad," "justice," "injustice," "democracy," and "communism." The third realm, the logological, deals with "words about words," and concerns grammar, etymology, literary criticism, poetics, rhetoric, and the like. The fourth realm, which Burke calls the "ultimate," is that of words for the mystical, divine, spiritual, or supernatural. Since, by definition, the supernatural is the realm of the ineffable, our words for this realm are borrowed analogically from the other realms (Burke, 1966, pp. 373–376; 1969a, p. 506; 1969b, pp. 183–189; 1970, pp. 14–15).

The ultimate hierarchical appeal is to move out of this world to the supernatural (Duncan, 1968, p. 80). The greatest distinction the human mind is capable of "is that between the sacred and the profane or merely utilitarian. . . . To endow anything with sacred significance . . . is to remove it from the sphere of things which must be justified by expediency or pragmatic considerations" (Nisbet, 1975, p. 87). In "I Have a Dream" King's appeal is based on the highest principle humans recognize, that of the supernatural realm. Mundane and/or sociopolitical actions are infused with higher meaning. By building a terministic bridge from marching and demonstrating for integration, equality and justice in the sociopolitical realm, to the supernatural or ultimate realm, King transcends the lower realm and places it within the context of the higher realm.

By examining the words which King clusters with his ultimate god-term "freedom," we can see how he achieves transcendence, how he moves "freedom" from the dialectical realm to the supernatural realm. According to Berthold (1976) there are five ways in which terms may be clustered with one another: (1) through conjunctions, (2) through cause–effect relationships, (3) through the use of mutual imagery, (4) through mutual connection to a third term, and (5) from the way they are used in a particular context (p. 306). In the first half of the speech King is mostly operating in the dialectical or sociopolitical realm, and the term "freedom" is used in that sense. Here "freedom" is clustered with "justice" (five of the seven uses of the word "justice" come in the first half of the speech), a sociopolitical term. As noted in chapter 3, "justice" is the *telos* of the social order. "Freedom" and "justice" are linked through conjunction—"the riches of freedom and the security of justice"—as well as through context: the demonstration is "*for* freedom" and "justice" is repeatedly invoked as one of the demonstrators' demands. The two terms are also linked through mutual imagery. The Emancipation Proclamation *freeing* the slaves was "a great beacon *light* of hope" and "justice" is a "*sunlit* path" and a "*bright* day." "Freedom" is also clustered with other sociopolitical terms in the first half of the speech. "Freedom" clusters with "equality" through conjunction: "an invigorating autumn of freedom and equality." "Freedom" also clusters with the sociopolitical term "democracy" through mutual connection to "justice": "Now is the time to make real the promises of democracy. . . . Now is the time to rise . . . to the sunlit path of racial justice. . . . Now is the time to make justice a reality for all of God's children" (M. L. King. 1963d, p. 724). "Freedom" and "justice" also cluster with "rights" and "the unalienable rights of life, liberty, and the pursuit of happiness" through context. Thus, in the first half of the speech "freedom" is repeatedly invoked as the goal of the demonstration, but the term is used mainly in the sociopolitical sense through its association with sociopolitical terms such as "justice," "democracy," "equality," and "rights," before the movement up the hierarchy to the supernatural realm which is fully developed in the second half of the speech.

Other analysts of this speech have also noted a shift in style and substance from the first half of the speech to the second half. Leff (1987) argues that King moves from historical time and up/down imagery in the first half of the speech to a time beyond history and images of ideal equality in the second half. Miller (1989) finds that King replaces "secular authority" in the first half of the speech with "divine authority" in the second half (pp. 27–28). But, King actually *begins* to build his terministic bridge up the hierarchy to the supernatural realm in the first half of the speech, and he builds his bridge in the Burkean sense by moving up, and then back down the hierarchy several times. Thus, the lower realm terms become "infused by the spirit" of the higher realm (Burke, 1970, p. 37). The first movement upward occurs about one-third of the way through the speech. King had just spoken of "the fierce urgency of now" and warned against gradualism, when he said:

> Now is the time to make real the promises of democracy.
>
> Now is the time to rise from the dark and desolate valley of segregation to the sunlit path of racial justice.
>
> Now is the time to lift our nation from the quicksands of racial injustice to the solid rock of brotherhood.
>
> Now is the time to make justice a reality for all of God's children. (M. L. King, 1963d, p. 724)

The "Now is the time" refrain connects making "real the promises of democracy" in the first line, to making "justice a reality for all of God's children" in the last line, while the two lines in between speak of "ris[ing]" from "segregation" to "justice," and "lift[ing]" ourselves from "injustice" to "the solid rock of brotherhood" (a phrase with spiritual connotations). The total image is one of upward movement (movement up a hierarchy) in which fulfilling the "promises of democracy" is in accord with God's will. Here King has begun to relate fulfillment of political justice in historical time to fulfillment of spiritual justice in God's time. King is beginning a repetitive form (Burke, 1968a, p. 125) of movement up the hierarchy from the sociopolitical to the supernatural, which he sometimes uses delivery to enhance. D. H. Smith (1964) has noted that the common pattern of King's delivery was to begin slowly, then gradually quicken his cadence, taking his audience up, then down again, through a series of miniclimaxes which build toward a final, driving climactic peroration. After each miniclimax King reverts back to his calm delivery to begin developing a new idea and prepare for the next climax, with each new series building toward his peroration (pp. 331–332). Generally, the minor climaxes are introduced by four or five repeated phrases, as in the "Now is the time" refrain cited above.

After the "Now is the time" refrain King reverts back to a more measured delivery. He warns the nation not to "overlook the urgency of the moment" and then cautions African Americans against violence or "distrust of all white people" (M. L. King, 1963d, p. 724). Four paragraphs after the "Now is the time" refrain, King begins another miniclimax, moving up the hierarchy:

> There are those who are asking the devotees of civil rights, "When will you be satisfied?" We can never be satisfied as long as the Negro is the vic- [*sic*] victim of the unspeakable horrors of police brutality. . . . We cannot be satisfied as long as the Negro's basic mobility is from a smaller ghetto to a larger one. . . . We cannot be satisfied as long as a Negro in Mississippi cannot vote and a Negro in New York believes he has nothing for which to vote.
>
> No, no, we are not satisfied, and we will not be satisfied until justice rolls down like waters and righteousness like a mighty stream. (M. L. King, 1963d, pp. 724–725)

This section again displays the repetitive form of anaphoric, hierarchical movement upward as King moves through a series of sociopolitical references that then conclude with words from the Old Testament prophet Amos.

In the next paragraph King first uses the word "faith," a term belonging to the supernatural realm, and clusters that term with "freedom" as he again moves up the hierarchy, this time without the use of anaphora or accelerating cadence:

> I am not mi- [sic] unmindful that some of you have come here out of *great trials and tribulations*. Some of you have come fresh from narrow jail cells. Some of you have come from areas where your crest- [*sic*] quest for *freedom* left you battered by the *storms of persecution* and staggered by the winds of police brutality. You have been the veterans of *creative suffering*. Continue to work with the *faith* that *unearned suffering is redemptive.* [emphases mine] (M. L. King, 1963d, p. 725)

Here King takes material and sociopolitical terms such as "narrow jail cells" and "police brutality" and associates them with concepts such as "great trials and tribulations," "persecution," "suffering," and "freedom"—terms which can function in the sociopolitical realm, but also have spiritual connotations—and then associates them all with the strongly spiritual terms "faith" and "redempt[ion]." King relates the struggles of civil rights workers in the here and now to their ultimate redemption.

In the next paragraph King comes back down again to secular language, naming particular states:

> Go back to Mississippi, go back to Alabama, go back to South Carolina, go back to Georgia, go back to Louisiana, go back to the slums and ghettos of our Northern cities, knowing that somehow this situation can and will be changed. Let us not wallow in the valley of despair. (M. L. King, 1963d, p. 725)

However, this paragraph also builds slightly toward an implied divine authority when King says "knowing that somehow this situation can and will be changed." This phrase contains implications of faith in an ultimate order, and the final sentence's "valley of despair" connotes the Twenty-third Psalm's "valley of the shadow of death" and other Biblical references to valleys as low points in the Christian journey toward salvation.

In the next paragraph King introduces the word "dream": "I say to you today, my friends, so even though we face the difficulties of today and tomorrow, I still have a dream. It is a dream deeply rooted in the American dream." The term "dream" is again taking us up to the mystical and supernatural realm, as in the dreams and visions of noted biblical figures such as Joseph. Parman (1991) has shown that the Judeo-Christian tradition in Western culture has regarded the dream as a bridge to the supernatural (pp. 27–45). King has made an explicit connection (built a bridge) between the "American dream" (sociopolitical term) and his "dream" as a vision of the future (ultimate term). Also, here King is moving out of the present, and out of real time, into the future, and into mythological time. The use of past–future themes in rhetoric is a mode of transcendence (Payne, 1989, pp. 97–108). King is achieving temporal transcendence by transcending the past and the present for the future. As King is passing from the material realm to the sociopolitical realm to the ultimate realm, he is also moving from the world of physical motion, time, and place—"we shall always march ahead"; "[s]ome of you have come fresh from narrow jail cells"; "[g]o back to Mississippi, go back to Alabama"—to the world of action and idea—"justice," "American dream"—to the world of unitary principles—"faith," "redemption," "dream" (see Burke, 1969b, pp. 183–187).

The final third of the speech (from the beginning of the "dream" sequence to the conclusion) is the long, consummating climax for which the speech has become famous. Here King stays in the ultimate realm. He has stepped out of real, historical time and into the impressionistic, utopian future. Although there are secular references, as I will demonstrate shortly, they are so tightly woven into the fabric of King's mythical/supernatural vision that they merge into it. By going up, then down, then up again from the positive realm, to the dialectical realm, to the ultimate realm, through several miniclimaxes that come closer and closer together, by the time of the final climax the secular terms have become "infused by the spirit" of the supernatural realm. For the remainder of the speech the sociopolitical terms "justice" and "equal[ity]" are used only once each, and they are now clustered with the supernatural terms "dream" (employed nine times, excluding the reference to the "American dream"), "faith" (four times, in addition to the previous use noted above), and "hope" (used twice), all put into the divine context as King draws upon biblical language in describing his "dream that one day every valley shall be exalted, every hill and mountain shall be made low, the rough places shall be made plain and the crooked places shall be made straight, and the glory of the Lord will be revealed, and all flesh shall see it together" (M. L. King, 1963d, pp. 725–26). In the conclusion, "freedom," the overarching god-term of King's message, is no longer only sociopolitical freedom, it is also spiritual freedom, spiritual redemption. It is clustered not with "justice," "rights," and "democracy," but with "dream," "faith," and "hope." It is linked with mountains, symbols of ascension and majesty, often associated with God in biblical literature. It is significant to note also, that in the first half of the speech where "freedom" clusters with the dialectical terms "justice," "democracy," and "rights," the linkage is most often through conjunction, cause and effect, mutual imagery, and mutual connection to a third term. Whereas in the final one-third of the speech, where "freedom" becomes supernatural and is linked to "faith," "hope," and mountain imagery, the link is almost entirely contextual through the organizing metaphor of the "dream" as a vision of a redeemed future (see chapter 5 on the analysis of the "dream" as metaphor). Before closely examining the final one-third of the speech, I must briefly explain why King needed to use a transcendent strategy.

Miller (1989) has suggested that King "replac[es] secular authority" in the first half of the speech with "divine authority" in the second half (pp. 27–28). But what King does is not so much *replace* secular authority with divine authority as *subsume the former under the latter*. That is, he transcends the secular order for the spiritual order. King's rhetorical strategy is a transcendent one because he had to reconcile two conflicting political/temporal tensions—white gradualism and black radicalism. Burke (1984a) notes that transcendence is the adoption of a perspective that allows one to merge opposites (p. 336). King reconciled the opposition between white gradualism and black radicalism by elevating the discourse to the moral/spiritual plane where this tension is transcended in a futuristic vision that subsumes historical time and political justice under eschatological time and spiritual justice. While King must convince his white audience that gradualism is not a fitting response to racial injustice, he has a separate rhetorical challenge with regard to his black audience. A people responding to injustice with nonviolence and dignity must have the hope that their virtue will be rewarded. Black radicals claimed that King's nonviolent methods were not working, or that they would take too long even if they did work. On this point the black radicals prevailed as long as the debate was conducted within the temporal dimension of history and political reality, so King transcended political justice and historical temporality for spiritual justice and eschatological temporality. Nonviolence was not only a political strategy, but also a redemptive act: "Continue to work with the faith that unearned suffering is redemptive." This was the only response King could give to the charges that nonviolence was ineffective. *In other words, he re-*

sponded to those charges by measuring the effectiveness of nonviolence not in political terms but in spiritual terms. He changed the terms of the debate with black radicals on how to achieve justice by subsuming the notion of political justice under one of spiritual justice. Nonviolence and love is not abandoned as a political strategy, but its political significance is subsumed within its greater spiritual significance. Thus King was reconciling divisions within his large national audience by elevating the discourse to a higher plane. The final third of the speech is King's elevated vision that subsumes all racial, temporal, and political oppositions under the banner of secular/spiritual redemption.

King achieves this reconciliation by transcending the sociopolitical realm for the supernatural realm while at the same time transcending political ideology for secular mythology. Burke (1947) argues that one way to transcend social and political differences is to move from the plane of ideology to the plane of myth (p. 198). As argued in chapter 3, America's most enduring myth has been its image of itself as a chosen people deposited in a virgin land to build a new order based on freedom, justice, and democracy. Thus, the final third of King's speech not only symbolically affects spiritual redemption, but also secular redemption by invoking American mythology and tying the fulfillment of that mythology into spiritual redemption. King's "dream" sequence depicts a nation that has risen up "to live out the true meaning of its creed" to provide freedom and equality for all. The myth of "the American dream" is invoked in a vision that extends that dream to black people as well as white people:

> I still have a dream. It is a dream deeply rooted in the American dream.
>
> I have a dream that one day this nation will rise up to live out the true meaning of its creed: "We hold these truths to be self-evident that all men are created equal."
>
> I have a dream that one day on the red hills of Georgia the sons of former slaves and the sons of former slave owners will ba- [sic] be able to sit down together at the table of brotherhood. (M. L. King, 1963d, p. 725)

In vivid language King envisions a series of transformations taking place in America:

> I have a dream that one day even the state of Mississippi, a state sweltering with the heat of injustice, sweltering with the heat of oppression, will be transformed into an oasis of freedom and justice.
>
> I have a dream that my four little children will one day live in a nation where they will not be judged by the color of their skin but by the content of their character.
>
> I have a dream that one day, d-o-w-n-n in Alabama, with its vicious racists, with its governor having his lips dripping with the words of interposition and nullification, one day right there in Alabama little black boys and black girls will be able to join hands with little white boys and white girls as sisters and brothers.
>
> I have a dream today! (M. L. King, 1963c; 1963d, p. 725)

In the final third of the speech King is masterfully merging spiritual redemption with secular mythology. The dream sequence depicts a series of utopian, mythical images—"the sons of former slaves and the sons of former slave owners" sitting "down together at the table of brotherhood;" and "little black boys and black girls . . . join[ing] hands with little white boys and white girls as sisters and brothers"—set within a series of secular references—"one day on the red hills of Georgia"; "one day even the state of Mississippi"; "one day, d-o-w-n-n in Alabama, with its vicious racists, with its governor having his lips dripping with the words of interposition and nullification"—which are then climaxed with a merging of the language of the Old Testament prophet Isaiah with King's own dream—"I have a dream that one day every valley shall be exalted, every hill and mountain shall be made low, the rough places will be made plain and the crooked places will be made straight, and the glory of the Lord shall be revealed, and all flesh shall see it together" (M. L. King, 1963c; 1963d, p. 725–726).

After this description of his "dream" King says that he will "go back to the South" with "hope" and "faith":

> This is our *hope*. This is the *faith* that I will go back to the South with. With this *faith* we will be able to hew out of the mountain of despair a stone of *hope*. With this *faith* we will be able to transform the jangling discords of our nation into a beautiful symphony of brotherhood. With this *faith* we will be able to work together, to *pray* together, to struggle together, to go to jail together, to stand up for *freedom* together, knowing that we will be *free* one day. [emphases mine] (M. L. King, 1963d, p. 726)

Working, struggling, and going to jail for "freedom" are here put alongside prayer, and all are clustered under acts of "faith." King does not explicitly say what or whom this "faith" is in, but from the context (the previous paragraph concluded with the words from the prophet Isaiah), it is almost certainly faith in some divine or supernatural order. When King concludes this paragraph with "*knowing* we will be free one day" [emphasis added], he communicates a sense of ultimate determinism, of long-term inevitability. "[O]ne day" could mean "one day" in historical time in this world, or "one day" in eschatological time in heaven.

Next, King merges the secular mythology of song lyrics from "America the Beautiful" with a reference to unity in God:

> This will be the day . . . when all of *God's* children will be able to sing with new meaning: "My country 'tis of thee, sweet land of liberty, of thee I sing. Land where my fathers died, land of the Pilgrims' pride, from every mountainside, let *freedom* ring," and if America is to be a great nation, this must become true. [emphases mine] (M. L. King, 1963d, p. 726)

The next section carries over the "let freedom ring" lyric into another refrain, combining it with secular references to well-known American mountain ranges. But, mountains in general also evoke the sense of Godlike vision from great heights. King calls for "freedom" to ring from mountains from east to west, paralleling the development of the nation, then finally south, the region where the greatest racial injustices were then being perpetrated.

> So let freedom ring. From the prodigious hilltops of New Hampshire, let freedom ring. From the mighty mountains of New York, let freedom ring, from the heightening Alleghenies of Pennsylvania!
>
> Let freedom ring from the snowcapped Rockies of Colorado!
>
> Let freedom ring from the curvaceous slopes of California!
>
> But not only that.
>
> Let freedom ring from Stone Mountain of Georgia!
>
> Let freedom ring from Lookout Mountain of Tennessee!
>
> Let freedom ring from every hill and mole hill of Mississippi. (M. L. King, 1963d, p. 726)

The final paragraph then explicitly reinvokes divine authority and climaxes King's "dream" within the spiritual context:

> From every mountainside, let *freedom* ring, and when this happens . . . when we allow *freedom* [to] ring, when we let it ring from every village and every hamlet, from every state and every city, we will be able to speed up that day when all of *God's* children, black men and white men, Jews and Gentiles, Protestants and Catholics, will be able to join hands and sing in the words of the *old Negro spiritual, "Free at last! Free at last! Thank God Almighty, we are free at last!"* [all emphases mine] (M. L. King, 1963d, p. 726)

The freedom here referred to is no longer only worldly, sociopolitical freedom; it has become infused with the spirit of the ultimate realm. "Freedom" now connotes national and spiritual rebirth and secular/religious redemption. King has transcended all racial and religious divisions for his listeners by moving up the hierarchy to the "'unitary principle' behind the diversity of voices" (Burke, 1969b, p. 187). By doing so, the struggle for racial justice in the sociopolitical realm is no longer only that. It is now also a divine struggle. It is not just a struggle for socioeconomic freedom, but also a struggle for spiritual freedom, for spiritual rebirth and a new identity for the individual and the nation. America, by living up to its secular promises, by bringing to realization its secular myths, has been assured of national redemption in the eyes of God. In King's vision of the future (his "dream") America's guilt has been purified and its people united under a transcendent, mythic ideal.

CHANGE, MOVEMENT, AND DRAMATIC CATHARSIS

Victimage, mortification and transcendence are not the only means whereby a rhetor may achieve symbolic purification for the audience. Due to its nature as arising out of the symbolic resources of language, purification may be accomplished via many symbolic modes (Rueckert, 1982, p. 137). Victimage and mortification are Burke's most frequently mentioned modes of purification, and Burke explicitly, although less frequently, mentions transcendence as a mode of purification, but he implicitly or briefly alludes to other means of purification as well. The following modes are not necessarily fully developed in Burke's theory, but are treated here in order to fill out the analysis of how King achieves symbolic purification, and to further demonstrate the many methods of purification available. Symbolic purification is a complex and subtle process. Many major and minor modes are possible; these often overlap, intersect, and loop back upon one another.

Rueckert (1982) notes that in Burke's theory "Purification is always a process—movement and change—something is always expelled or sloughed off, and the end is always a change of some kind, whether physical, spiritual, or psychological. Of necessity, purification is almost always depicted by 'active' or 'process' images" (p. 104).

Hoban (1980) argues that rhetorical rituals of rebirth use images of transformation and metamorphosis—expressed as temporal, spatial, or psychological change—to "provide a purifying basis for a new order" (p. 285). According to Rueckert (1982), among the many images Burke treats as producing purification through change and movement are the following: fire; journeys, pilgrimages, and quests; "movement of any kind from negatively charged to positively charged, such as . . . night to day, down to up"; the "act of unburdening or divesting" of any form; "imagery of ascent (mounting)"; and dying and killing (p. 105).

King's "Dream" speech is rich in imagery of change and movement, especially in its metaphors. In his study of archetypal metaphors in the light–dark family, Osborn (1967a) notes that change can be represented by seasonal metaphors (p. 124); we can observe King's use of this imagery when he speaks of the "sweltering summer of the Negro's legitimate discontent" to be followed by an "invigorating autumn of freedom and equality" (M. L. King, 1963d, p. 724). Throughout the speech, King's metaphors and images create a sense of change and continuous movement, forward and upward:

> Now is the time to *rise* from the dark and desolate valley of segregation to the sunlit path of racial justice. Now is the time to *lift* our nation from the quicksands of racial injustice to the solid rock of brotherhood. . . . Again and again

> we must *rise* to the majestic *heights* of meeting physical force with soul force. . . . And as we walk, we must make the pledge that we shall *always march ahead*. We cannot turn back. [all emphases added] (M. L. King, 1963d, p. 724)

In addition to change and movement, some metaphors can contain specific purifying images in themselves. For example, Osborn (1967a) notes that rebirth can be symbolized by dawn metaphors (p. 121) and we see King's use of such images in the following phrases: "It [the Emancipation Proclamation] came as a *joyous daybreak* to end the long night of their captivity"; and "The whirlwinds of revolt will continue to shake the foundations of our nation until the *bright day* of justice emerges" [emphases added] (M. L. King, 1963d, pp. 723, 724). Fire metaphors can represent purifying or purgatorial forces (Osborn, 1967a, p. 123), and we note King's depiction of "Negro slaves, who had been *seared in the flames* of withering injustice" [emphasis added] (M. L. King, 1963d, p. 723). Water is also a purifying element. The following phrase combines images of purification through water, as well as movement: "and we will not be satisfied *until justice rolls down like waters and righteousness like a mighty stream*" [emphases added] (M. L. King, 1963d, p. 725).

Not only are images of change and movement elicited by King's use of metaphor, his "dream" sequence speaks of a series of changes or transformations from the present reality to a future order. He sees the state of Mississippi, "a state sweltering with the heat of injustice, sweltering with the heat of oppression . . . *transformed* into an oasis of freedom and justice"; and the state of Alabama, "with its vicious racists" transformed into a place where "little black boys and black girls will be able to join hands with little white boys and white girls as sisters and brothers." King also speaks of the faith that will enable us "to *transform* the jangling discords of our nation into a beautiful symphony of brotherhood" [emphases added] (M. L. King, 1963d, pp. 725, 726).

Burke (1973) finds that in *The Grapes of Wrath* Tom Joad's journey serves as a type of "pilgrim's progress" for the redemption of his crime (p. 82). In King's speech the depiction of America's historical journey in search of its destiny amounts to a type of "pilgrim's progress" for the nation as a whole. It is a national quest of purpose, a chronological account of America in search of its true identity. King's references early in the speech to the Emancipation Proclamation, the United States Constitution and the Declaration of Independence refer to America's past and its basic myths and values embodied in those documents. The historical journey is brought up to the present where America has failed to live up to these promises "insofar as her citizens of color are concerned." In the dream sequence King takes us into a future utopia where America has risen up to "live out the true meaning of its creed;"

that is, where the purpose of America has been realized in the extension of the American dream to all its people and the nation has been redeemed. This historical journey of America in quest of its purpose is parallel to the journey of the individual soul from innocence to sin to redemption. Spillers (1971) writes in "I Have a Dream" King's images of struggle and journey through valleys and mountains provide an "allegory of the Christian journey" (p. 25).

The American/Christian journey King depicts is a type of drama, with the forces of good and the forces of evil doing battle for the soul of America. Drama or symbolic conflict can also provide catharsis for the audience (Burke, 1966, pp. 186–191). The cluster-agon analysis presented in chapter 3 showed that the protagonist in King's speech is "freedom," and its satellite terms are "justice," "equality," "democracy," etc., while the antagonistic cluster consists of the terms "injustice," "segregation," "discrimination," and "vicious racists." Thus the protagonists, the god-terms of "freedom" and "justice," are in conflict with the antagonists, the devil-terms of "injustice," "discrimination," and "racism," for the soul of America.

Rueckert (1982) notes that cathartic drama releases "civic tensions" (p. 211), and Burke (1966) talks about this taking place through symbolic sacrifice of an appropriate victim (pp. 88–89, 189). A victim or scapegoat, who assumes the burden of "unwanted evils," can be considered appropriate or worthy in many ways, such as "by making him an offender against legal or moral justice, so that he 'deserves' what he gets" (Burke, 1973, pp. 39–40). According to Duncan (1968), guilt can be purged through witnessing or participating in a social drama in which we symbolically banish, punish, or kill somebody or something which personifies evil (pp. 140–141). In King's "drama," racists and segregationists are the scapegoats for society's ills, and civic tension (or guilt) over racism and segregation is released as these sources of corporate pollution are symbolically killed or expunged from the body politic. Perera (1986) notes that ceremonies for the riddance of collective guilt operate by expelling what is felt to be alien. In such a case "the restoration of a sense of wholeness" depends upon "a consciousness-fostering ritual of separation from evil by collective confession and sacrifice" (p. 12). In King's dramatic conclusion the protagonists, the "good guys," have won out. His "dream" includes no place in the reborn America for the racists and segregationists. They have been eliminated, or purged, from his vision of America's future. The scapegoat is "dialectically appealing" because it "combines in one figure contrary principles of identification and alienation" (Burke, 1969b, p. 140). Thus listeners who identify a part of themselves with racism and segregation receive catharsis through vicarious victimage, and those who see racism and segregation as outside themselves but part of the body politic, see it alienated and symbolically killed.

In sum, King's multiple images of change, movement, and transformation, as well as the depiction of dramatic conflict between good and evil, resolved in favor of the forces of good, vividly reinforce the process of symbolic purification taking place through victimage/mortification and transcendence.

REDEMPTION

As noted earlier, for purposes of persuasion, purification is the most important part of the guilt-purification-redemption cycle. It is the fulcrum of the process of movement from guilt to redemption. Redemption is a temporary state at the end of the cycle before it repeats (on redemption, see Burke, 1970, pp. 4–5, 174–178; Foss, Foss, and Trapp, 1985, p. 181; Rueckert, 1982, p. 131). Rueckert (1982) describes redemption as:

> [A] moment of stasis, the still moment following the fusion and release of a symbol-induced catharsis, or the still moment of vision when, after the furious activity of dialectic, a fusion at a higher level of discourse takes place to produce a perceived unity among many previously discordant ideas and things. (pp. 137–138)

Burke (1966) observes that "the cleansing of guilt must be contrived in ways that reinforce the very assumptions on which the sense of guilt was based" (pp. 351–352). Thus, we note that King's "dream" amounts to a description of a type of heaven on earth, a state of national rebirth or redemption in which the very sources of America's guilt—hierarchy, failure to live up to the ideals of justice and equality for all, racial discrimination, etc.—are eliminated. In their place is an America of freedom, justice, and brotherhood. America's rebirth is indeed a rebirth, for it is a new order that finally realizes the dreams and promises contained in America's past. King's description of this redemptive state is consistent with America's most basic values and positive myths about itself. America has risen up (been reborn) to "live out the true meaning of its creed."

Burke (1973) notes that "symbolic rebirth" can be provided through a "'positive' view of life" such as can be gotten through a feeling "of *moving forward*, towards a *goal*" [emphases in original] (p. 203). King's speech gives the listeners the sense that America has a destiny to fulfill, a great purpose she is moving toward. King's listeners partake of that purposefulness. For the advocates of civil rights, the marchers and demonstrators, their actions are imbued with a higher meaning. All guilt is purged and their commitment to the cause is further inspired. For moderate white America, their guilt is also purged if they symbolically join the movement. They can be reborn and redeemed by joining the movement, forward and upward towards the goal—an

America of freedom, justice, and racial harmony. In the new America King envisions, racism and segregation have been expunged, purifying the body politic and allowing national redemption to take place. Thus, King's redemption drama creates a stasis of attitude in the auditor. Burke (1969a) notes that an attitude can either be "an incipient act or the substitute for an act" (p. 476). King's speech could be an incipient act if it emotionally prepares the audience for action, or it could be a "substitute for an act in that the sympathetic person can let the intent do service for the deed" (p. 476). In chapter 7 I will argue that one of the long-term effects of this speech has been that it provided our culture with a discursive artifact that has been used more for the latter than the former. But King's purpose was to create the conditions for an act of purification to allow redemption and reconciliation to take place. A type of temporal movement is posited by King which corresponds to the tripartite pentadic ratio analysis and narrative form (representative anecdote) analysis presented in chapter 3. A past of racial injustice is transformed by an incipient purificatory action that results in future redemption. Adding this temporal dimension to the diagram from chapter 3 gives us a schematic representation of the speech that looks like this:

Pentadic Ratio	scene	act	purpose
Narrative Form	guilt	purification	redemption
Temporal Movement	past	present	future

"Temporal Movement" is not to be understood in terms of the actual structure of the speech (although the speech does roughly follow this pattern), but in terms of the attitude King was attempting to instill. "Temporal movement" is King's proposed temporal movement in which the present is not the actual, immediate present, but the incipient present of the act of purification and the past is the guilt-ridden scene that America is about to shed. The following chapter on metaphoric analysis will, among other things, demonstrate how this tripartite structure is reinforced in King's metaphors.

5

Metaphoric Analysis

Martin Luther King's "I Have a Dream" speech is dense in metaphor. In order to attain a fuller understanding of the speech and to see how his metaphors contribute to the overall dramatic enactment examined in the previous chapters, it is necessary to analyze King's metaphors. First, a brief history of the theory of metaphor is presented to show how metaphor, once regarded by most theorists as a simple stylistic device, has come to be regarded as a language phenomenon with important epistemological implications. Then I. A. Richards' interaction theory of metaphor, as extended by Paul Ricoeur and others, is discussed. Here I also demonstrate why this theory is superior to others as an analytical tool for allowing the critic to unpack the underlying meaning, or truth claims, implicit in a metaphorical expression. Edwin Black's concept of the second persona is also used because Black argues that the study of a rhetor's metaphors provides a means of determining how the rhetor defines the role the audience plays in the social drama depicted by the discourse. Finally, these theories are used to analyze King's major metaphoric clusters in "I Have a Dream." In the discussion of purification in chapter 4 I briefly illustrated the purificatory effects of some metaphors used by King, but this chapter presents a more thorough analysis of King's metaphors from the perspective of contemporary metaphorical theory.

A BRIEF HISTORY OF THE THEORY OF METAPHOR

Throughout most of the history of its study in Western rhetoric, literature, and philosophy the metaphor was regarded by most theorists as simply an ornamental trope that substituted one term for another in conveying an idea in a lively or unusual way. But twentieth-century theorists have come to regard the metaphor as a way of thinking, as a device that makes an argument in its own behalf (see Burke, 1984b, pp. 89–96; Ivie, 1987, p. 166; Osborn and Ehninger, 1962, pp. 223, 233; Richards, 1936, pp. 89–112; for overviews of the history of the theory of metaphor, see Osborn, 1967b; and Ricoeur, 1977). Thus, observes Whitson (1989): "The metaphor has gained much importance of late. No longer simply a decorative feature of discourse, the trope has obtained an epistemological and ontological dimension. No longer merely a figural flourish of prose, the metaphor has acquired an important role in the study of human understanding" (p. 253).

Aristotle's *Rhetoric* and *Poetics* were the first texts to treat the theory of metaphor in some detail (*Rhetoric*, Book III, chapters 2–4 and 10–11; *Poetics*, chapter 20 and 1459a 5–8; for a thorough analysis of Aristotle's theory of metaphor, see Ricoeur, 1977, pp. 9–43). Aristotle defined metaphor as "giving the thing a name that belongs to something else; the transference being either from genus to species, or from species to genus, or from species to species, or on grounds of analogy" (*Poetics* 1457b 6–9). According to Johnson (1981), Aristotle's definition of metaphor established the metaphor as (1) a transference between words, rather than at the level of the sentence, (2) a deviation from literal usage, and (3) based on similarities between things (pp. 5–6). Aristotle's theory of metaphor is usually seen as establishing the view of metaphor as a stylistic device which substitutes one name for another, a view which persisted and grew until the medieval period when metaphor came to be regarded as simply an ornamental trope which substituted one term for another to convey an idea in a lively or unusual way (see Johnson, 1981, pp. 8–11; and Ricoeur, 1977, pp. 44–48). However, Aristotle's writings do contain hints that he recognized metaphor's epistemic role. For example, in *Rhetoric* (1410b 5–11) he maintains that "ordinary words convey only what we know already," but it is through metaphor that we can "best get hold" of a "new idea": "When the poet calls old age 'a withered stalk,' he conveys a *new idea, a new fact*, to us by means of the general notion of 'lost bloom,' which is common to both things" [emphasis added]. (For an interpretation of Aristotle's theory of metaphor which stresses the epistemic aspect of Aristotle's theory, see Derrida, 1982, pp. 236–245.)

Although the view of metaphor as a stylistic device that simply substitutes one word for another dominated until the twentieth century, some rhetorical theorists and philosophers apparently did recognize metaphor's ability to function epistemically. Osborn (1967b) argues that the view of metaphor as a category of thought evolved "in a slow, growing realization" in post-Renaissance Western thought. He finds nascent hints of such a view in the writings of Lord Kames, George Campbell, and others. Johnson (1981) argues that an exception to the dominant view of metaphor was Kant's insight that the metaphoric capacity is one aspect of our ability to create new concepts that cannot be captured in literal expression (p. 14). Another exception to the dominant view, Nietzsche (2001), saw metaphor as basic to the process of human intellection. He maintained, "the drive toward the formation of metaphors is the fundamental human drive, which one cannot for a single instant dispense with in thought" (p. 1177). Nietzsche argued that all language formation itself is metaphoric. Thus, when we speak of things, "we believe that we know something about the things themselves," but our words are "nothing but metaphors for things." The concepts we accept as "truths" are nothing but "metaphors that have become worn out" (p. 1174).

In *Permanence and Change* (originally published in 1935) Kenneth Burke was one of the first twentieth-century theorists to maintain that metaphor has a heuristic and epistemic role. In functioning as a "perspective by incongruity" it brings together terms from different categories of association and thereby allows us to see heretofore unrevealed relationships (Burke, 1984b, pp. 89–96). Burke tied metaphor to motives through his concept of "perspective" (see Ivie, 1988). A "perspective" is a point of view or a general orientation for the interpretation of reality (Burke, 1984b, pp. 5–14). Motives are linguistic explanations or justifications for conduct based upon the accepted norms of our language group, and are thus assigned with reference to our orientation or perspective (Burke, 1984b, pp. 19–31). Therefore, *motives* are a subset or result of our *perspective* (pp. 25–31), and metaphors provide perspective: "Metaphor is a device for seeing something *in terms of* something else. . . . to consider A from the point of view of B is, of course, to use B as a *perspective* upon A" [emphases in original] (Burke, 1969a, pp. 503–504). Burke (1973) further maintained that "[e]very perspective requires a metaphor, implicit or explicit, for its organizational base" (p. 152, n. 2). According to Burke (1966), symbolicity itself contains a perfectionistic tendency or "compulsion" toward carrying out the "implications of one's terminology" (p. 19). All words, including metaphors, function as "terministic screens," filters through which we view reality. Much of what "we take as observations about 'reality' may be but the spinning out of possibilities implicit in our particular choice of terms" (Burke, 1966, p. 46; also see Crusius, 1999, pp. 58–63 and pp. 128–133). Thus, metaphor is more than a decorative device for an idea. Metaphors imply truth claims. By organizing "perspective" and providing "screens" through which to view the world, they function as ways of depicting reality. The unpacking of the meaning contained in a metaphor can reveal the epistemic claim implied by the metaphor.

Richards (1936) maintained that metaphor is an "omnipresent principle" of language and thought: "*Thought* is metaphoric, and proceeds by comparison, and the metaphors of language derive therefrom" [emphasis in original] (pp. 92–94). Like Burke, Richards also realized that metaphor raises significant epistemological issues. The processes of metaphoric creation and the exchanges between meaning and metaphor are "super-imposed upon a perceived world which is itself a product of earlier or unwitting metaphor, and we shall not deal with them [metaphors] justly if we forget that this is so" (pp. 108–109). Richards also made an important break from the traditional view of metaphor as a process of describing a resemblance or similarity between objects by pointing out that many metaphors depend upon a relationship of *dissimilarity* or *disparity* between objects, thus creating a *new meaning by creating or positing a heretofore unseen similarity* (pp. 107–108). I will return to Richards' theory of metaphor shortly when I discuss the interaction theory of metaphor which was originated by Richards, but for now I will continue with the discussion of twentieth-century theories of metaphor to illustrate the role modern metaphor theory has ascribed to metaphor in describing and creating reality.

For Grassi (1980), also, metaphor plays a central role in the process of thought and meaning creation. For him metaphor is not only an interaction between two objects, but is basic to the process of *ingenium*. *Ingenium* is the fundamental and primary mode of human thought. It is the grasping of original insight as invention and discovery of ideas, relationships, and premises (pp. 7–8, 91–92). Thus, *ingenium* precedes deduction, because one can only draw deductive conclusions from premises or insights one has already grasped (pp. 45–46). According to Grassi, this capacity for original insight is the metaphoric process, because truly original ideas can only be expressed in metaphors: "The metaphor is, therefore, the original form of the interpretative act itself, which raises itself from the particular to the general through representation in an image" (p. 7). Note the similarity of Grassi's theory to those of Kant and Nietzsche discussed above, who all see metaphor as basic to the process of the discovery and articulation of original concepts.

Hayden White also sees metaphor as integral to the discovery of original insights. He further argues that metaphor can be the first step in the creation of patterns of discourse and meaning-formation. White (1978) begins by maintaining that the study of the human sciences relies on tropes: "[T]ropics is the process by which all discourse *constitutes* the objects which it pretends only to describe realistically and to analyze objectively" [emphasis in original] (p. 2). Since understanding is the process of making familiar the unfamiliar—that is, of moving from the domain of unclassified experience to that of encoded, accepted associations—it necessarily requires the process of troping. Thus, the process of understanding proceeds by exploitation of the four master tropes—metaphor, metonymy, synecdoche, and irony (White,

1978, p. 5). (On the four master tropes, also see Burke, 1969a, pp. 503–517.) Therefore, White believes that the "archetypal plot of discursive formations" moves from "original metaphorical characterization of a domain of experience, through metonymic deconstructions of its elements, to synecdochic representations of the relations between its superficial attributes and its presumed essence," to, finally, ironic detachment and reflection on the inadequacy of the characterization itself to include all elements of the reality it is supposed to represent, or even to "self-reflexivity on the constructivist nature of the ordering principle itself" (pp. 5–6). White does not claim that this pattern of tropological prefiguration is universal, but that it does recur persistently in modern discourse. According to White, a historian's choice of a governing metaphor becomes a heuristic rule that determines what will be considered as historical data (pp. 46–47). In sum, in a manner similar to that of Grassi and Nietzsche, White sees metaphor as the initial characterization that establishes the framework for the construction of patterns of human consciousness and meaning-creation.

Philosophers of language have noted the relationship between metaphor and the polysemic nature of language. For Foucault (1972), the polysemic nature of language renders a statement neither completely visible nor completely hidden. Language, after its "meaning" is extracted always contains leftover meaning—a "proliferation of thoughts, images, or fantasies." Thus, an "analysis of statements can never confine its attention to the things said, to the sentences that were actually spoken or written, to the 'signifying' elements that were traced or pronounced" (p. 109). It must also consider the leftover meanings that have left traces, awaiting the moment when they might be used again. Because of the polysemic nature of language all statements contain a profusion of meanings, some of these obviously metaphoric.

Ricoeur's (1973) analysis of creativity and polysemy in language treats metaphor as a "creative use of polysemy and in that way a specific strategy of language. Instead of reducing or suppressing polysemy, metaphor uses polysemy as a means to preserve polysemy and to make it work in a most effective way" (p. 105). When we accept a metaphor as meaningful "we perceive both the literal meaning which is bound by semantic incongruity and the new meaning which makes sense in the present context." Metaphor is a "clear case where polysemy is preserved instead of being screened." Two lines of interpretation are open at the same time and put into tension. Thus, several layers of meaning now dwell in the words themselves (p. 110). Moreover the relationship between metaphor and polysemy is one in which metaphor creates and extends polysemy. Once a metaphor is accepted by the language community, it tends to become literal. "Then it is merely added to the previous polysemy of the word. In this way we may say that metaphor is the procedure by which we extend polysemy" (Ricoeur, 1973, p. 110). I will present more on Ricoeur's theory of metaphor in the section on the interaction theory, which Ricoeur has extended. But before moving on to the interaction theory and its application to King's speech, I will mention the work of some rhetorical critics and theorists who have made use of and developed the new approaches to metaphor.

Rhetorical theorists have advanced the argument that metaphors provide prisms through which we interpret reality, thus directing action. In other words, metaphors can provide the linguistic frame through which actors perceive and deal with a situation (see Ivie, 1987, p. 166; Leff, 1983, pp. 219, 222–223). For example, Ivie (1982) demonstrates how a particular metaphor can become literalized in use. That is, the element of analogy is forgotten and the metaphor dominates the discourse to the degree that it excludes all other perspectives. Carpenter's (1990) study shows how the "frontier" metaphor of American westward expansion has been transferred and updated to fit new situations Americans have encountered in the Spanish-American War, World War I, World War II, the Cold War, and Vietnam. These subsequent American challenges were thus framed as extensions of the American frontier experience. The metaphor establishes a "terministic incentive" by providing the nomenclature that "necessarily directs the attention into some channels rather than others" (Burke, 1966, p. 45). Osborn's (1967a, 1977) work has demonstrated how the use of archetypal metaphors such as "the sea" and light/dark imagery can establish structures of meaning in discourse (light/dark imagery in "I Have a Dream" is discussed briefly in chapter 4 and will be discussed more extensively later in this chapter). The work of Ivie (1980, 1987) and Jamieson (1980) on how metaphoric clusters can be studied to identify the patterns of meaning constituted by a rhetor will be discussed later in this chapter.

In sum, contemporary theories of metaphor reject the traditional view of metaphor as the substitution of a figurative or poetic term for a literal expression, the purpose of which being to "dress up" an idea or make it more vivid, for a view which sees metaphor as part and parcel of the process of rhetorical invention and meaning creation. As Osborn (1967b) summarized the contrast between the two views: "Metaphor, instead of being selected after and apart from the discovery of ideas, occurs anterior to, and actually generates, the discovery of ideas" (p. 130).

THE INTERACTION THEORY OF METAPHOR

Many of the strands of modern theories of metaphor come together in the interaction theory of metaphor, which provides a methodology for ascertaining the meaning structures implied by a particular metaphor. The interaction view of metaphor was first presented by I.A. Richards in 1936. In *The Philosophy of Rhetoric* he maintained that "when we use metaphor we have two thoughts of different things active together and supported by a single word, or phrase, whose meaning is a resultant of their interaction" (Richards, 1936, p. 93). Metaphor, then, is a "borrowing between and intercourse of *thoughts*, a transaction between contexts" [emphasis in original] (p. 94). Richards' theory is a significant advance over the classical concept of metaphor in two respects. First, it is a movement away from the idea of the *substitution of one word for another*, and toward the idea of metaphor as the *bringing together of two contexts of meaning* (p. 93). When a metaphor is used it is more than the exchange of one word for another. It is the bringing together of two entire realms of association. Secondly, Richards realized that the *interaction* between the two contexts *creates an entirely new meaning*, "a meaning of more varied powers" than could be ascribed to either alone (p. 100). Richards also greatly simplified our terminology for the parts of the metaphor and facilitated analysis by introducing the terms "tenor," for the principal subject or original idea, and "vehicle," for the borrowed idea or metaphoric image (p. 96). (For analyses of Richards' theory of metaphor, see Johnson, 1981, pp. 18–19; and Ricoeur, 1977, pp. 76–83).

Max Black (1962) extended Richards' interaction theory. Rejecting the substitution theory, that a metaphor is used in place of some equivalent literal expression (pp. 31–34), and the comparison view, that metaphor is a presentation of an underlying analogy or similarity (pp. 35–37), Black argues that metaphor "has its own distinctive capacities and achievements" and that in some cases it "creates" a similarity rather than formulating an antecedently existing one (p. 37). Black endorses Richards' interaction view: in metaphor two thoughts "are 'active together' and 'interact' to produce a meaning that is a resultant of that interaction" (p. 38); the reader is forced to "connect" the two ideas (p. 39). Black further argues that metaphor works by applying to the tenor a system of "associated commonplaces" or accepted implications that are characteristic of the vehicle (pp. 40, 44). Any characteristics of the tenor that can be understood in terms of the vehicle will be foreground, or "rendered prominent." The tenor, then, is "seen through" the vehicle (p. 41). Thus, the metaphorical meaning emerges as the two interact with one another and various aspects of each are selected, emphasized, or suppressed according to what makes sense in the particular context (see Leff, 1983, p. 217).

Max Black's work added to Richards' interaction theory by explaining how the context of meaning of the vehicle gives rise to new meaning in the tenor. By virtue of its "associated commonplaces"—that is, by virtue of the preconceptions and ideas associated in the linguistic community with the vehicle—

the vehicle acts as a filter or screen to organize our view of the tenor. In this way it confers "insight" (see Ricoeur, 1977, p. 87). However, Black's notion of "associated commonplaces" only considers connotations that are already established (see Ricoeur, 1977, p. 88). Thus we are left with a type of substitution theory—although an advance over the original—in which we have merely exchanged "associated commonplaces" for the word itself. Beardsley's (1962) work resolves this difficulty by pointing out that metaphorical meaning need not depend on *actual* properties of its objects, but often acts at the level of sense or meaning: "the metaphor transforms a *property* (actual or attributed) into a *sense*" [emphasis in original] (p. 302). As the metaphor is employed in other applications in its new sense, it is not only actualizing an existing connotation, but establishing a new one (p. 302). Thus, a metaphor may not only "thrust latent connotations into the foreground of meaning," but bring "into play some properties that were not previously meant by it" (p. 303). In this way, metaphor is actualizing meanings not yet present in our conceptual system. (For an analysis of Beardsley's theory of metaphor, see Ricoeur, 1977, pp. 90–98.)

The interaction theory of metaphor is an advance over the classic substitution theory in three respects. First, it recognizes that words themselves are not metaphoric. Words are only metaphoric within the context of a sentence or a larger body of discourse (Ricoeur, 1973, p. 106). Second, the interaction theory recognizes that a metaphor has to pose a tenor against a vehicle. It is the unity, or the tension, of the two within the context of the discourse, which creates metaphorical meaning (Ricoeur, 1973, p. 106). And third, with the contributions of Black and Beardsley, the interaction theory recognizes that it is not merely a matter of comparing objects to determine which properties applying to one also apply to the other, but instead that an entire system of associative meanings (both preexistent and those newly created by the metaphorical interaction) is being used to filter or organize some other system (Johnson, 1981, p. 28).

Thus, according to Ricoeur, within this new framework, metaphor's predicative and epistemological character is revealed. For Ricoeur, more directly than any other theorist, the problem of metaphor is connected to the issue of the relationship between truth and reality. The meaning of metaphor ultimately turns on the question of predication; that is, what is meant by the copula "to be." Thus, the study of metaphor raises questions of ontology, epistemology, and metaphysics. The metaphoric utterance exploits access to a network of predicates in a familiar field of reference. This already constituted meaning is taken from its initial field and cast into a new referential field in which it functions to delineate meaning. This transfer requires the receptive field to be already present in an unarticulated manner that exerts an attraction on the already constituted field of meaning to tear it away from its initial haven. It is therefore in the semantic scope of the initial (unarticulated) field that the energy required to make the transfer resides. This transfer would not be possible if meaning were stable (Ricoeur, 1977, p. 299). Metaphor thus relies upon a purposive semantic discrepancy in which two semantic fields collide. The metaphoric attribution is the construction of a network of interactions as the resultant contradiction, and its semantic resolution, create new meaning (Ricoeur, 1973, p. 106; 1977, pp. 98–99). Metaphorical meaning "does not merely consist of a semantic clash but of the *new* predicative meaning which emerges from the collapse" of the common, usual meaning [emphasis in original] (Ricoeur, 1978, p. 146). It is in this moment of imagination, what Ricoeur (1978) calls the insight of "predicative assimilation" that new meaning is born (pp. 147–148). In metaphor, "to be" is used in a nonliteral, nondenotative, thus transcendent, sense. The distinction between literal and figurative sense, and denotative and connotative meanings, are false dichotomies for Ricoeur. Literal usage is just figurative usage that has become accepted as conventional (Ricoeur, 1977, pp. 229–231, 236–237, 290–291, 296–297). Therefore, according to Ricoeur (1977) the "place" of the metaphor is not in the word, the sentence, or even in the discourse, but in the copula of the verb *to be*: "The metaphorical 'is' at once signifies both 'is not' and 'is like,'" giving metaphorical reference the power to "redescribe reality" (p. 7). This is why Ricoeur (1977) rejects the dissociation of a theory of resemblance from the interaction theory of metaphor (pp. 173–215). For him, resemblance is even more necessary in an interaction theory than in a substitution theory. The predicative attribution of metaphor is an attribution of similarity or resemblance, the resemblance of "seeing as." But, the resemblance of "seeing as" is "no longer the resemblance between two ideas, but that very resemblance 'seeing as' establishes" (p. 213). In other words, it is the predicative resemblance of the metaphoric attribution (see pp. 188–190, 194).

Thus, Ricoeur's extension of the interaction theory into the realm of predication opens epistemology to metaphoric intervention, raising questions concerning the relationship between language and reality. The underlying issue of Ricoeur's work is, as Johnson (1981) notes, whether reality is objectively given, so that we can only stand apart and comment upon it, "or whether we have a 'world' only by virtue of having a language and system of value-laden concepts that make experience possible" (p. 41). Ricoeur's theory sees metaphor as a way of making and experiencing our world and gives metaphor an epistemological dimension. We experience the world not passively, but by means of projecting our thought system (through language and metaphor) upon it.

THE SECOND PERSONA

I will shortly examine the major metaphors in King's "I Have a Dream" speech to determine how his tenors and vehicles interact to produce meaning, to redescribe reality. However, there is one more aspect of modern theories of metaphor that requires examination. In a sense, Edwin Black's (1970) essay, "The Second Persona," introduced to the field of rhetorical criticism the modern reconceptualization of metaphor. Black argues that there is a reciprocal relationship between the language a rhetor uses and his or her thinking or "inner state" (p. 110). Furthermore, the discourse not only implies something about the author, if it is accepted by the auditor it also implies an "ideology" and a role for the auditor—that is, "the second persona" (pp. 111–113). Black writes: "Actual auditors look to the discourse they are attending for cues that tell them how to view the world" and, the "critic can see in the auditor implied by the discourse a model of what the rhetor would have his real auditor become" (p. 113). As a paradigmatic example Black examines the "cancer of communism" metaphor in the discourse of the "Radical Right" to see what such a metaphor implies about the worldview of the audience that attends to that discourse. Black concludes by suggesting that there are "strong and multifarious links between a style and an outlook" and that the critic may legitimately "move from the manifest evidence of style to the human personality that this evidence projects as a beckoning archetype" (p. 119). If, indeed, metaphors have the power to "redescribe reality" as Ricoeur asserts, then the acceptance of a rhetor's metaphors would be an acceptance of his or her description of reality. Booth (1978) argues: "To *understand* a metaphor is by its very nature to *decide* whether to join the metaphorist or reject him, and that is simultaneously to decide either to be shaped in the shape his metaphor requires or to resist" [emphases in original] (p. 65). For Booth, so strong is this link between the acceptance of a metaphor and acceptance of the reality it posits, that he maintains "the quality of any culture will in part be measured both by the quality of the metaphors it induces or allows and the quality of the judges of metaphor that it educates and rewards" (p. 64). Thus, the concept of the second persona will allow the metaphoric analysis to be extended to the second person, so to speak, to determine the implied role assigned to the auditors by their acceptance of King's metaphorical world.

METAPHORIC CLUSTERS

The sheer number of metaphors in the "Dream" speech makes a detailed analysis of each one a daunting task. As Leff (1987) has stated, the metaphors in the "I Have a Dream" speech "are so diverse and so densely packed that, when examined in detail, they tend to bewilder the critic rather than to yield insight into the structural integrity of the text" (pp. 1–2). However, an analysis in terms of King's metaphoric clusters, or his system of associated metaphorical concepts, will yield a better understanding of how King's metaphors contribute to the overall meaning of the text than would a study of particular metaphors as if they are unrelated phenomena. The concept of metaphoric clusters has been employed by Ivie (1980; 1987), Jamieson (1980), and Solomon (1993). Ivie (1980) points out that the *topoi* a rhetor may call upon form "associated clusters." The *topoi* used to generate a constellation of meaning can be studied to identify the "strategies by which discourse is infused with rhetorical appeal" (p. 282). The critic can arrange a rhetor's vehicles into subgroups by clustering those containing similar concepts (Ivie, 1987, p. 167). Jamieson (1980) argues that "metaphors simultaneously create inventional possibilities and impose inventional constraint." Adopting a particular metaphor involves the rejection of others and entails the spinning out of consistent metaphors within that cluster (p. 54). She contends that by examination of recurrent patterns of metaphoric usage "critics can minimize the likelihood that they are generalizing from aberrant rhetorical cues" (p. 51).

There are three main metaphoric clusters in King's "I Have a Dream" speech. First, early in the speech there is King's extended "check/promissory note" metaphor. In King's prepared text this metaphor provides a major theme early in the speech around which King intended to emphasize the overdue obligations America owed to its citizens of color (see C. S. King, 1969, p. 236; M. L. King, 1963b; Solomon, 1993). Second, King employs a number of metaphors of the type Osborn (1967a) has termed "archetypal." These are metaphors based on basic and prominent features of human experience, thus transcending time and culture. Examples of archetypal metaphors include water and sea metaphors, dark/light images, down/up images, and mountain and valley metaphors. Some of these images have been commented upon in the previous chapter. However, dark/light imagery, because of its association with what is the most significant natural cycle humans experience, the daily rising and setting of the sun, is perhaps the most important archetypal metaphor. Dark/light imagery is at the center of a cluster of metaphoric images King employs involving dichotomies of down/up, backward/forward, and bound/free. Third, the metaphor of the "dream" is quite significant in this speech. The "dream" sequence is the climactic moment of the speech and the passage for which the speech is named and remembered. "Dream" is King's metaphor for his vision of the future (of the beloved community), which, as we saw in the previous chapter, is the transcendent moment of the speech in which King elides social and political differences for his audience. Therefore, I will examine three metaphoric clusters in King's "I Have a Dream" speech: (1) the "check/promissory note" cluster; (2) the use of dark/light metaphors and its associated clusters; and (3) the "dream" cluster. My procedure will be threefold. First, using the interaction theory of metaphor (as extended by Ricoeur and others) presented earlier in this chapter, I will examine each metaphoric cluster to determine what is the vehicle's predicative attribution with regard to the tenor. That is, what perspective is the auditor being invited to adopt, what reality is King describing through his selection of metaphors? Second, applying the theory of the second persona, I examine the metaphors to determine what role the discourse assigns to the auditor who accepts King's metaphoric world. And third, in conjunction with the above and with the analysis presented in the previous chapters of King's speech as a guilt-purification-redemption drama, I consider the relationship of the metaphoric clusters to one another and to the text as a whole.

I contend that when we examine the relationship among King's three main metaphoric clusters we will see that they maintain and reinforce the structural integrity of the text's guilt-purification-redemption form. First, the "bad check" metaphor occurs early in the speech. A bad check conveys the idea of an unpaid obligation, of something owed to someone. This corresponds to the guilt phase of the redemption drama for whites (although it does reinforce the purification through victimage element for blacks). Second, most of the dark/light imagery, and its associated metaphors of down/up, backward/forward, and bound/free occur in the middle third of the speech (although some do occur early in the speech, these are mostly "bound" images which reinforce the element of guilt and prepare the way for movement to the second term of the above pairings). This imagery conveys the sense of struggle between evil and good and between injustice and justice, and of movement, forward and upward, or from dark to light or bound to free. This corresponds to the purificatory phase of the redemption drama. In the final third of the speech the contrasting metaphors (dark/light, down/up, bound/free, etc.) are almost completely absent. The final third of the speech is dominated by images that portray events on a higher and mystic plane ("dreams" and mountains) and on an even level, where the vision of equality is being described (Leff, 1987, makes this same point). This corresponds to the redemptive phase of the redemption drama.

THE CHECK/PROMISSORY NOTE CLUSTER

Early in his speech King uses the extended metaphor of a "check" or "promissory note," around which he clusters a series of financial/legal terms, to describe the rights to which black people have been entitled but denied:

> In a sense we've come to our nation's capital to *cash a check*. When the architects of our Republic wrote the magnificent words of the Constitution and the Declaration of Independence, they were *signing a promissory note* to which every American was to fall heir. This *note was a promise* that all men—yes, black men as well as white men—would be guaranteed the unalienable rights of life, liberty, and the pursuit of happiness. It is obvious that America has *defaulted on this promissory note* insofar as her citizens of color are concerned. Instead of honoring this sacred obligation, America has given the Negro people a *bad check*, a *check* which has come back marked "insufficient funds." But we refuse to believe that the bank of justice is bankrupt. We refuse to believe that there are insufficient funds in the great vaults of opportunity of this nation. So we've come to *cash this check*—a *check* which will give us upon demand the riches of freedom and the security of justice. [all emphases mine] (M. L. King, 1963d, pp. 723–24)

My approach in examining this extended metaphor or analogy is twofold: first, what type of metaphoric interaction is taking place between the vehicle and the tenor—that is, what is the vehicle predicating about the tenor; and secondly, what does the metaphor imply about the second persona—that is, what is the worldview and role of the audience?

The tenor of this metaphor is the rights owed to African Americans. The vehicle, of course, is the check or promissory note, the later being a financial obligation to pay a certain amount of funds at a specified time. The metaphor predicates social and political rights in financial/economic terms. In other words, King is using a financial vehicle to describe a moral and political obligation. This metaphorical attribution presents several problems. When money is owed, one can pay the sum owed, with interest, and the debt is canceled, but making good on a moral or political obligation is more difficult. The main implication of the check/promissory note vehicle is one of financial and legal specificity. Checks and promissory notes state precisely what is owed and exactly when and how it is to be paid. A check is "made good" by paying a specific amount in dollars upon presentation of the check to a proper financial institution. There are certain easily completed, commonly known procedures for cashing a check. For example, one will need to endorse it and often show identification. Furthermore, once a check is paid, it is "paid in full." There is no outstanding balance and it is easy to determine if the amount due has been paid in full.

Thus, if the rights owed to African Americans are like a check or promissory note, several implications follow. We are precisely sure what those rights are and we can easily determine if they have been paid in full. We know exactly what is owed and specifically to whom. The procedure for "cashing in" upon those rights is a routine and relatively simple task. However, "rights" such as "life, liberty and the pursuit of happiness," "justice," and "freedom" are amorphous and ill-defined concepts. Their nature is continually being worked out in the American legal and political process. There is no point at which one can say those "rights" have been guaranteed or "paid in full." There is no simple, routine procedure for "cashing in" upon such fluid concepts as "justice" and "liberty." Thus, King has employed a simplistic, quantifiable economic metaphor to organize the auditors' perspective on a complex, non-quantifiable situation. A complex social/moral obligation involving rights which are as yet unsecured (and for which there is as yet no national consensus as to the specific nature of that obligation) is being predicated in terms of something as quantifiable and routine as cashing a check. When money is owed one can pay the amount owed and the debt is canceled, but how does one pay back a moral or political obligation? The metaphor attempts to predicate a moral claim of social justice in terms of a specific financial obligation.

Another predication of this metaphor concerns the relationship of a victim to an institutional authority. "Checks," "promissory notes," "banks," and "vaults" are symbols of institutional authority and order—specifically financial institutions that harbor and safeguard resources. The "check" is supposed to give one access to those resources. But, if it is a "bad check" which has come back marked "insufficient funds," if the institution has "defaulted" on the "promissory note," then one has been cheated. Thus one is a victim. And the victim is still owed something. To have received a "bad check," or to be the victim of an unmet financial obligation, is to be the victim of one more wily and powerful than oneself (at least in the context of the way King weaves this metaphor, with references to institutional authority). This reinforces the concept of inequality between the races, with blacks as the victim and whites as the institutional authority that has cheated on its "promise," on its "sacred obligation." The victim is morally superior to the victimizer. This metaphor thus reinforces other allusions in the speech to white guilt, and black purification through being a victim (see chapters 3 and 4), as well as reinforcing King's subtext of reconciliation through an exchange of black moral authority for white socioeconomic authority (see chapter 7).

What does this metaphor of the check/promissory note imply about the second persona? When King speaks about "the bank of justice" and "the great vaults of opportunity of this nation," he tells his auditors that those rights are just sitting there in abundance (earning interest?) and that they can be simply handed over "upon demand." What role does that imply for the auditor? The auditor is one who presents her check to the bank, receives her payment and goes away and spends her money. It is an essentially passive role. In King's metaphor, the "cashing in" on "rights" is a simple, quick transaction, when in fact the guaranteeing of rights is a complicated, long-term, active process.

In sum, although people play a role in agitating for and demanding their rights, once the "bank" recognizes its obligation to pay, the "rights" can be simply handed over and there is no further dispute about what is owed to whom. Those rights can now be freely and easily exercised—once one has cashed a check, the money can be freely and easily spent. There is no further obligation on the part of the bank and no further right to demand payment on the part of the payee. Such a metaphor implies that the rights to be won are clear and specific, the procedures of transaction will be quick and quotidian, and that the exercise of those rights will be easy and routine. Thus, King's check/promissory note metaphor contributes to the elision of social and political differences among his hearers that is evident in the transcendent nature of his rhetoric in this speech, and possibly to the ultimate disappointment of African Americans when the legal victories of the first phase of the civil rights movement failed to produce easy and immediate socioeconomic equality. Just as King's redemption drama asks for no action on the part of his hearers, only that they have "faith" in the vision, this metaphor implies that we only need to have faith that once America recognizes its moral obligation, the previously withheld rights can be simply handed over, presumably with interest, and all will be well. While King may have hoped to create a sympathetic attitude for an incipient action, this particular metaphor predicates an attitude that substitutes intent for action (see Burke, 1969a, p. 476).

THE DARK/LIGHT CLUSTER

The second metaphoric cluster to be examined in King's "Dream" speech is dark/light imagery and its associated, dichotomous down/up, backward/forward, and bound/free imagery. All these metaphors involve good versus bad antitheses, images of positive versus negative force, and/or movement from the first term of the pair to the second. These metaphors feature prominently in the speech, mainly by connecting "injustice," "segregation," or "discrimination" with darkness—or the first term in one of the above dualities—and "justice," "freedom," or "equality" with light—or the second, positive, term of the pair.

For example, early in the speech King combines dark/light and bound/free images when he tells his listeners that the Emancipation Proclamation "came as a great beacon *light* of hope to millions of Negro slaves who had been seared in the flames of withering injustice. It came as a joyous *daybreak* to end the long night of their *captivity*" [all emphases added] (M. L. King, 1963d, p. 723). In the next paragraph King exploits a series of "bound" vehicles to depict the current situation of blacks in America:

> [T]he Negro is still sadly crippled by the *manacles* of segregation and the *chains* of discrimination . . . lives on a *lonely island of poverty* in the midst of a vast ocean of material prosperity . . . is still *languished* in the corners of American society and finds himself an *exile* in his own land. [all emphases added] (p. 723)

After establishing the deplorable nature of blacks' condition in America with his "bound" vehicles, and then the use of the check/promissory note metaphor discussed above to communicate obligation, King returns to the dualistic metaphors of the dark/light cluster, but this time with images of movement from the negative terms of the pairs to the positive terms. "Now is the time to *rise* from the *dark and desolate valley* of segregation to *sunlit path* of racial justice. Now is the time to *lift our nation* from the *quicksands* of racial injustice to the *solid rock* of brotherhood" [all emphases added] (p. 724). In the next two paragraphs the movement from negative to positive images is used again:

> This *sweltering summer* of the Negro's legitimate discontent will not pass until there is an *invigorating autumn* of freedom and equality. . . . The whirlwinds of revolt will continue to shake the foundations of our nation until the *bright day* of justice emerges. [all emphases mine] (p. 724)

Black people are then described, in a combination of forward movement and light imagery, as "stand[ing] on the *warm* threshold which *leads* into the palace of justice" [all emphases added] (p. 724). ("Warmth" is part of the "light" family of associations; see Osborn, 1967a, p. 122.) The next two paragraphs make use of down/up and backward/forward imagery, communicating the ideas of movement and determined struggle toward a worthy goal:

> We must forever conduct our struggle on the *high plane* of dignity and discipline. We must not allow our creative protest to *degenerate* into physical violence. Again and again we must *rise to the majestic heights* of meeting physical force with soul force. . . . And as we walk, we must make the pledge that *we shall always march ahead. We cannot turn back.* [all emphases mine] (p. 724)

Thus, we see King employing a cluster of dualistic vehicles for injustice and segregation on the one hand, and justice, freedom, and equality on the other hand, occurring mostly in the middle third of the speech (between the end of the "check/promissory note" cluster and the beginning of the "dream" cluster) which make use of contrasts between, and movement from, negative to positive images, as well as spatial movement forward and upward. This metaphoric cluster, through its use of images of change, movement, and struggle between good and evil (or between positive and negative forces) complements the purification stage of the redemption drama (see chapter 4).

What are the implications of the use of this metaphoric cluster? What does this type of language predicate about the civil rights movement? Darkness connotes nighttime, blindness or difficulty in seeing, and fear of the unknown. Light is associated with sight, with warmth, with daytime; in short, positive things. Obviously dark/light imagery can be a powerful rhetorical device for speakers who want to associate one thing with positive values and its opposite with negative values. However, Osborn (1967a) finds further rhetorical implications of such imagery. First, dark/light images "indicate and perpetuate simplistic, two-valued, black-white attitudes which rhetoricians and their audiences seem so often to prefer"; it "simplifies complex situations and facilitates choice" (pp. 117, 118). Thus, while King's metaphors associate "justice" with light and positive values, and "injustice" with darkness and negative values, they also reinforce the simplistic thinking about complex social issues that we saw in his check/promissory note metaphor, but this time cast in the frame of binary antithesis. The distinction between injustice and justice is as clear as the distinction between night and day. For the auditor, the choice is simple and the values are absolute. There is no in-between, no shades of meaning, no degrees of justice or injustice—"you are either part of the problem or part of the solution," as a popular saying of the 1960s went. Thus, King's dark/light imagery helps effect the polarization of the audience into those who are saved (those who are redeemed, those who have "seen the light") and those who are lost (racists). In King's transcendent vision, one either accepts the transcendent values of the social order, or one mires in sin and rebellion. The individual (and the nation) is either destined for a secular heaven or condemned to the hell of racial injustice and segregation. The other metaphors in this cluster—down/up, backward/forward, bound/free—also reinforce thinking in terms of two-valued, simplistic dichotomies. For example, in King's metaphoric world, one is either "bound" or "free." "Freedom," however, is not an absolute, but always a matter of degree. All human beings who are part of a social order have restrictions on their freedom. These metaphors eschew thinking in terms of moral and social complexity in favor of binary antithesis. A metaphoric cluster centered around images of evolutionary progress probably would have been more descriptive of how social change actually occurs, and perhaps proved less disappointing to adherents of the movement when its moral and legal victories did not immediately catapult African Americans from bound, down, and dark injustice to a world of freedom, equality, and justice. Metaphors of evolutionary progress might not have been as effective in the short run, but might have better sustained the movement for the long run than did dualistic metaphors promising a utopian world of freedom and equality. A treatment of the civil rights movement in more complex terms might have better prepared it to deal with the imperfect accomplishment of its goals than did the treatment of issues in terms of two-valued dichotomies.

Second, Osborn (1967a) notes that dark/light images carry with them a sense of inevitability or determinism. The inevitable cycle of nature is that day follows night. Dark/light imagery, by associating the present with darkness and the future with light, carries with it implications of the routine, determined spinning of the earth (pp. 117–119). In King's address, if "justice" is inevitable, the situation is under the ultimate control of a higher power. It is the moral law of the universe. King had often told his audiences that "the universe is on the side of justice" (M. L. King, 1957a, p. 31) and that "God is with us in our struggle" (M. L. King, 1981, p. 65, 110). The idea of determinism and the inevitability of ultimate justice is reinforced by King's use of nature metaphors (changing seasons, flowing waters, valleys and mountains) and constant use of images of forward and upward movement.

In terms of the second persona, again, we see the reinforcing of an essentially passive role for the audience. There is no specific, active role for the audience to play beyond supporting its leaders in agitating for "rights" and "justice." The "rights" demanded are specific and easily provided, and the expected condition of "justice" is inevitable and clearly distinguishable from the present state of "injustice." The use of seasonal and nature metaphors strengthens the sense of determinism and inevitability, thus casting the auditor in an essentially passive role. In addition, dark/light, down/up, and backward/forward imagery, and nature metaphors, are nonspecific about political means and general about time. These metaphors set the stage for the transcending of social and political differences, and the reconstituting of real, historical time as mythic and supernatural time, in the final third of the speech.

THE DREAM CLUSTER

The final third of King's "I Have a Dream" speech is dominated by the image of the "dream." In his study of the metaphoric clusters in Henry Wallace's rhetoric, Ivie (1987) places "dream" as a vehicle in the dark/light cluster along with "light," "dawn," "vision," "nightmare," "down," "dark," and others (p. 170). While "dream" as a vehicle may often belong in a "light" cluster through its associations with vision and seeing, in this speech it belongs in a separate cluster. Not only does the "dream" vehicle form an organizing principle that dominates the final third of the speech, but it is also used in a manner different from the way the dark/light cluster was used in the middle of the speech. The dark/light cluster was used to express contrast between "injustice" and "discrimination" on the one hand, and "freedom" and "justice" on the other, and then struggle between and movement from the negative term to the positive term of each antithetical pair. In the final third of the speech the element of contrast, struggle, and movement is considerably lessened as King speaks more from an elevated plane envisioning a world in which freedom, justice and equality have been achieved. As Leff (1987), who divides the speech into two halves, puts it, the first half is dominated by down/up patterns of strife, while in the second half, it "is as though King has risen to a high plateau where everything is even and on the same level" (p. 3) and where "a condition of strife gives way to fixed, timeless principles of equality" (p. 6).

The "dream" vehicle also poses a slightly different problem of analysis than the previous metaphors in the speech because it has two different senses. A dream is a series of mental images that occur in a state of sleep. However, "dream" can also mean an aspiration, an ambition, or a hope, as in "the American dream." The latter is clearly the sense in which King meant to cast this metaphor. We can discern this from the total context of the speech, as well as the immediate context, where King says: "I still have a dream. It is a dream deeply rooted in the American dream" (M. L. King, 1963d, p. 725). "The American dream," of course, is a phrase used rather loosely for an individual goal or hope for "the good life" of work, family, independence, and financial security. So when King says: "I have a dream " he is essentially saying "I have a hope" or a "vision" for America that looks like this. But while "dream" has come to mean a hope, vision, or aspiration, it originally means a series of mental images occurring during sleep (see *Oxford English Dictionary*, Vol. 4, p. 1036). Therefore, in this case we have a vehicle with a double level of meaning: "dream" as mental images during sleep (level one) and "dream" as goal, vision, or aspiration (level two). Although from the context we can clearly discern that King meant "dream" in its level-two sense, the first-level implications are nonetheless inherent in the use of the term. As Richards (1936) points out, when we use a word, the other words in the language that overlap with it in sound and meaning form a part of the context for determining its meaning (pp. 62–63). Therefore, "dream" level two (as a hope or aspiration) always contains within it, as part of it, the sense of "dream" level one (as mental images in sleep). The latter is not extracted from the meaning of the former, but the former is grafted onto the meaning of the latter. So in this case we have a vehicle that has a double level of meaning, and both levels of meaning must be considered. Together, they facilitate King's attempt to elide social and political differences through transcendence to the mythic and supernatural realms.

"Dream" at its first level of meaning, as mental images occurring during sleep, bridges the conscious with the unconscious and the secular with the spiritual. White (1978) says that metaphor functions as a symbol rather than as a sign; it gives directions for finding the set of images it seeks to characterize. The metaphor does not suggest specific attributes, but that the tenor shares qualities that have come to symbolize the vehicle in customary linguistic usages of the culture (p. 91). In Western culture, dreams are commonly seen as a window to the unconscious mind, and in the Judeo-Christian tradition as the manner in which God sends a message or reveals his will to his servants (see Parman, 1991). Thus, "dream" (level one) predicates transcendence and communication between the consciousness and unconscious realms and the natural and supernatural realms. The implication of King's vision as a "dream" is that King has access to some transcendent realm of consciousness.

Hariman (1989) has noted other implications in King's speech associated with "dream" (level one). "Dream" as mental images during sleep is a vehicle which "takes us out of time. A dream by definition is not a part of real time. Dreams have no secure, measurable sense of duration; dreams regularly scramble time and still make sense" (p. 211). Thus, "dream," at its first-level meaning, is a vehicle which carries implications of uncertain duration, a scrambling of chronology and contexts, and of vaguely remembered images that occur in an unconscious or semiconscious state. While Hariman is basically correct about the nature of time in dreams, he is incorrect in saying that they "still make sense." In fact, dreams usually do not make much sense. They are difficult to recall and difficult to understand. Therefore, the predication of "dream" (level one) is of something of a vague and uncertain nature that takes place outside of real time. The implication of King's vision as a "dream" is that the auditor is left uncertain as to when and how this is supposed to take place. The "dream" of the racially just and harmonious society is a beautiful utopian vision, but time frames and specific political actions are neglected. Dreams are, after all, illusions, self-deceptions. They are phenomena which seem real when they are being experienced, but are in fact, not real. The English word "dream" comes from the old Germanic root word *draugmo*, which has two senses, the first meaning joy, mirth, or music, but in its second sense meaning deception or illusion (*Oxford English Dictionary*, Vol. 4, p. 1036). What role is the auditor to play in bringing about this vision? Again, the second persona is essentially passive.

"Dream" at its second level of meaning, as a vision or a hope for the future (as in the "American dream") invokes American mythology. Hariman (1989) notes: "King's dream evokes the American dream, that mythic celebration of prosperity for all achieved by individual initiative and effort. Again, we are pulled out of time and into those myths used to legitimate the status quo" (p. 211). What are the associated implications of the vehicle "dream" in this sense? The American dream is a national mythic construct—a Horatio Alger parable of prosperity through hard work and virtue. While this sense of "dream" does imply a more active role for the auditor (sort of a self-help, "pulling yourself up by your bootstraps" role), as Hariman notes, even at this level of meaning the "dream" vehicle pulls the audience out of real time and politics and into myth and legend. The vehicle provides no clue as to how or when this utopian vision is to be accomplished.

As I noted above, the "dream" metaphor dominates and organizes the final third of King's speech. As discussed in chapter 4, this is the part of the speech which is the most transcendent as King moves out of historical time and the sociopolitical realm and into mythic time and the supernatural realm. The "dream" metaphor, with its symbolization of American mythology, and its implication of transcendence to the supernatural realm, is perfectly suited as a vehicle for carrying the redemptive phase of King's guilt-purification-redemption drama. The "dream" metaphor allows King to function as visionary, as seer, of the new redemptive state. The "dream" vehicle predicates both American mythology ("the American dream") and communication with the supernatural realm, thus reinforcing the dualistic nature of the secular/spiritual redemption King has invoked (see chapters 3 and 4). This sense of King as secular visionary and mystic seer is reinforced by the other imagery used in this part of the speech. As discussed in chapter 4, King's expression "dream" is clustered with biblical language from the Book of Isaiah and then followed up with sentences employing the supernaturally suggestive terms "faith" and "hope," and with images of mountains. The images of mountains reinforce King's stance as a mystic visionary. Burke (1969b) says that mountains can be associated with the "mystical" (p. 302). Leff (1987) finds that by the end of the dream sequence, "as he recalls the words of Isaiah, King virtually assumes a stance of poetic or mystic reverie" (p. 7).

CONCLUSION

Because of the power of metaphor and word choice to shape human perception of reality, King's metaphors cannot be seen as neutral reflections of an already constituted meaning; they themselves predicate meaning and provide heuristic perspective, and thus direct action, on the issues with which King was dealing. King's choice of metaphors has several implications for the analysis of this speech.

First, King's metaphoric clusters are largely congruent with the guilt-purification-redemption form of the speech. King's metaphors move from: (1) images of black bondage, white guilt, and national obligation to fulfill its promises, to (2) purificatory images of struggle and movement from negative to positive terms, to (3) an elevated plane of meaning in which images of dreams and mountains are used to communicate a transcendent vision of equality, fulfillment of national promise, and secular/spiritual redemption. We can now add the metaphoric clusters to the diagram of the speech previously presented:

Pentadic Ratio	scene	act	purpose
Narrative Form	guilt	purification	redemption
Temporal Movement	past	present	future
Metaphoric Cluster	bound images/ bad check	struggle and movement within dark/light cluster	dream

Thus the bound images and the "bad check" metaphor in the first third of the speech predicate what King proposes as the immediate past scene of an America blighted by the guilt of racial injustice, which America is to leave behind. King's proposed act of purification in the incipient present is predicated through images of struggle between and movement from the first, negative term of the dark/light clusters, to the second, positive, terms of the metaphoric pairings, mostly occurring in the middle third of the speech. And finally, the "dream" metaphor organizes the final third of the speech in which King describes his futuristic vision of America fulfilling its purpose and achieving national redemption.

Second, King's metaphors characterize the issues of the civil rights movement in simplistic terms that avoid sociopolitical complexity and moral ambiguity. The check/promissory note metaphor puts the goals of the movement in terms of the clarity and specificity of a routine financial obligation, envisioning the attaining of justice as a straightforward task of redressing (redeeming) past wrongs by getting the government to honor its "check." This metaphor allowed King to give concreteness to the amorphous concept of "rights," but the vehicle implies that the "debt" can be "paid in full" and past racial injustice "redeemed" by an action on the part of the nation as simple as that of cashing a check. Furthermore, the issues of the movement are predicated in terms of two-valued antitheses between dark and light, bound and free, up and down, and backward and forward. This allowed King to cast the issues in terms of simple dichotomies of evil versus good, injustice versus justice, inequality versus equality, and so on. However, this also ignored the complexities of the issues and slighted the difficulties of achieving the goals of the movement. In light of the powerful impact of this speech on public consciousness, King's metaphoric choices may have inadvertently contributed to subsequent disappointment when the moral and legal victories achieved in the first phase of the civil rights movement failed to deliver immediate social and economic salvation for black Americans. A discourse of consensus building, emphasizing the consolidation of gains as one gradually moves forward in shaping a better, but still imperfect, world, might have avoided the impression that the ultimate goals of the movement could be directly realized with the passage of certain pieces of legislation. The black power advocates realized that full social and economic equality would not come immediately upon the recognition by white America of certain legal and political rights for black Americans (see chapter 7). King realized this later in his career, but this speech is the legacy he has been assigned, and the King of this speech, not the later King, is the King celebrated today as a national icon (see chapters 1 and 7; Dyson, 2000, pp. 14–18 makes the same point). The "dream" metaphor, while allowing King to provide hope and inspiration through a vision of a new, redeemed America, also contributed to the elision of social and political difficulties by taking the audience out of real time and history and by defining the goals of the movement in terms of American mythology. C. T. Vivian, a veteran of the sit-in movement and the Freedom Rides, who joined the SCLC staff in 1963, later felt that the civil rights movement's acceptance of America's myths about itself was among the chief reasons for the failure of the movement to achieve its goals beyond the dismantling of legal segregation. Vivian (1970) wrote that the movement had erred because it had acted upon the false assumption that it was dealing with a truly Christian and democratic nation that would live up to its principles once the injustices of racial discrimination and segregation were exposed (pp. 55–59, 68–122).

Third, King's metaphors define the audience, the second persona, in a generally passive role. There is little sense of the auditors as active, engaged agents in a process of continuous, ongoing, evolutionary change. The "check" vehicle casts the audience as receivers of a "payment" who then simply go out and "spend" their newly won rights. The dark/light cluster and the nature metaphors provide no defining role for the audience. The other parts of the speech do not provide any more of a proactive, decision-making role for the audience. The auditors are told to continue to march, to "work," to "pray," to "struggle," to "stand up for freedom . . . *knowing* that we will be free one day" [emphasis added] (M. L. King, 1963d, p. 726). But there is little sense of the audience as active agents who participate in and shape their own emancipation, beyond their role as the ground troops of the movement. This is consistent with the underlying Christian theme of King's message. In the Protestant Christian tradition one is saved not by works, but by faith. King's speech of national salvation is concerned not with means but with ends. The audience's main role is to have faith in the vision of salvation.

6

Evaluation of the Theory of Guilt-Purification-Redemption

Chapter 7 will examine the social and political implications of the foregoing critical analysis of King's "I Have a Dream" speech. But, the other purpose of this book is to develop Burke's theory of guilt-purification-redemption. Therefore, this chapter will confine itself to an assessment of the guilt-purification-redemption methodology to consider its value as a tool of rhetorical criticism applicable in other situations and consider the implications of the use of this rhetorical form.

Thus far Burke's theory of guilt-purification-redemption has been developed and applied to King's "I Have a Dream" speech, but the theory itself has not been critiqued to consider its usefulness in other contexts. In this chapter, I will examine what the findings of this study reveal about the explanatory power of the redemption methodology. I will consider the adequacy of Burke's theory of guilt, whether guilt is ontological, as Burke claims, and whether Burke's theory is still useful if guilt is not ontological. I also will examine what this study reveals about the Burkean modes of purification and suggest other modes that rhetorical critics should study. Finally, this chapter considers what the guilt-purification-redemption drama reveals about a culture that adopts and accepts this form as a way of experiencing and structuring reality.

CRITIQUE OF BURKE'S THEORY OF GUILT

In Burke's redemption drama the need for redemption is generated by an initial state of guilt, which Burke claims is inherent in humans as symbol-using animals. While in a particular situation—such as that in which King's

"Dream" speech took place—it may be relatively easy to demonstrate that guilt was a primary motivating factor, Burke's claim concerning guilt's ontological status is not the kind of claim that can be empirically proven. This section critiques Burke's concept of guilt, examines in what way guilt can be said to be ontological, and considers to what degree the guilt-purification-redemption methodology is useful as a tool of rhetorical criticism if guilt is not ontological.

Many people have trouble accepting the idea of guilt as ontological, as something part and parcel of our being. This may be due to the negative connotations we attach to the word "guilt." However, as was pointed out in chapter 2, the ontological nature of guilt has been noted by psychologists and philosophers (Buber, 1965; Carroll, 1985; Reik, 1957, pp. 41–43) and is a basic feature of much existential philosophy. For example, Heidegger (1962) claims that human beings "*are* guilty in the very basis of their Being" [emphasis in original] (p. 332). I will briefly examine Heidegger's theory of guilt, because while it is similar to Burke's in some respects, it differs in a way that allows a critique and improvement upon Burke's theory.[1] Heidegger (1962) argues that because Dasein's (Heidegger's term for human being, or what it is to be human) relationship to the world is one of "care" or intentional activity toward a world it finds itself thrown into, Dasein "constantly lags behind its possibilities" (p. 330). Built into Dasein's existence is its awareness of what it is not and its knowledge of its inability to transcend itself. This possibility for inauthenticity, Heidegger terms "nullity" (p. 331). Thus, he argues, "*Being*-guilty is more primordial than any *knowledge* about it. And only because Dasein is guilty in the basis of its Being . . . is conscience possible" [all emphases in original] (p. 332).

Heidegger's theory of guilt is similar to Burke's in several respects. Both find guilt to be existential, in the basis of our being, and both see conscience as arising out of existential guilt as opposed to the other way around (where conscience creates the condition for guilt), as is the usual understanding. Also, Heidegger's concept of guilt as based upon "nullity," Dasein's sense of what it is not, echoes Burke's concept of guilt resulting from the linguistic creation of the negative. However, where Heidegger finds guilt to be primordial and prelinguistic, Burke bases ontological guilt on symbolicity itself, where symbolicity is the defining characteristic of human beings. Burke's failure to recognize the prelinguistic nature of guilt is a shortcoming of his theory. If guilt were a result of human beings' inability to transcend themselves (Heidegger's "nullity"), then guilt would be prelinguistic. The basic condition of our existence is that we are (or exist in) physical bodies that are physically separate from others of our species and from the rest of the physical world. Burke is aware of this basic condition of human existence, and implies its relationship to guilt, but does not explicitly treat it as a cause of guilt. For example, Burke (1969b) discusses the fact that human beings are somewhat divided from one another, or are of both distinct substance and consubstantial with one another. Our shared substance makes communication possible, while our division makes it necessary. It is this desire to identify with one another, to transcend ourselves, which makes communication necessary (pp. 20–23). Burke does mention that this "simultaneous identification-with and division-from" results in the need for a scapegoat—a mode of purification—(p. 46), but fails to develop this connection to guilt, instead focusing in other works on guilt as a result of symbolicity. Burke misses the existential nature of physical separateness because for him "division" is treated mainly in its sociological, thus linguistic, aspect. It seems with Burke's definition of human beings as "bodies that learn language" he should not have missed the fact that our basic condition of existence is one of physical separation, but he chose instead to focus on shared aspects of humanity.

I do not want to use this argument for prelinguistic guilt to refute Burke's theory of guilt, but as an addendum to it. Guilt may be viewed as both prelinguistic and linguistic. Guilt is rooted in human nature because it is caused by that inevitable sense of division and separateness from others that resides in us as individual physical bodies who cannot have complete consubstantiality with other physical bodies. This sense of division is what we attempt to overcome through communication, although we can never overcome it completely. However, our attempts at overcoming division through the use of symbols to share meaning can also have certain guilt-inducing effects. For guilt to be an inevitable, recurring condition, it would need to be both prelinguistic and linguistic. If symbol use itself could completely overcome division (as prelinguistic guilt), then guilt would not be a recurring cycle. Through proper communication we could reach a point of stasis, of ongoing and possibly permanent redemption. Burke's contribution in pointing out the linguistic sources of guilt tells us why that does not happen.

In considering the claim of the ontological nature of guilt, we must be aware that both Burke and Heidegger are, in a sense, using the term "guilt" catachrestically—that is, for lack of a better term in the language to communicate the concept they want to communicate. They use the term "guilt" to mean more than the usual sense of guilt as a feeling of responsibility or shame for having done wrong. Guilt is that ontological sense of anxiety that comes with being human. There is no way to "prove" empirically that guilt is ontological, but the argument is logical, both in the sense of guilt as prelinguistic, discussed above, and in Burke's sense of guilt as arising out of our symbol-using nature. Language gives us the capacity to create standards and rules of behavior (what Burke calls the "thou-shalt-nots") as well as the capacity to conceptualize and communicate ideas of perfection, all of which cause guilt when not lived up to.

Another cause of guilt, according to Burke, is hierarchy. Language gives us a cultural matrix within which hierarchies are embedded, and hierarchy results in guilt. Radical egalitarians, such as some feminists and Marxist cultural critics, attack Burke on this point, maintaining that hierarchy is not inevitable. But a Burkean would respond that symbol use inevitably creates hierarchy. Once people start labeling and naming things and acts, distinctions and judgments are inevitable. A hierarchy is simply a distinction of some type, an act of assigning value. There is no example of a society that has not had some type of hierarchy. As Condit (1991) has noted, on the inevitability of hierarchy in human systems, "Burke's analysis has been shown to be largely correct; we have learned that even in noncapitalist systems, dominated by discourses of equality, hierarchies reappear" (p. 7).

There is a school of thought that would admit Burke's claims for the significance of guilt as a dominant motive in Western, Judeo-Christian culture, but deny its universality. For example, Condit (1991) argues that Burke's theory is ethnocentric because it draws mainly on Western texts and the Judeo-Christian religion. "It may be that the cycle of guilt-victimage-purification-redemption is the single strongest motive in American discourse. But I believe we have insufficient evidence to claim that it is the *dominant* motive of *all* cultures" [emphases in original] (p. 5). Condit does not deny the *possibility* of guilt as a motive in other cultures, but simply questions Burke's claim of its universal dominance. While the widespread occurrence of rites of purification in non-Western cultures (see Frazer, 1911–1915; Perera, 1986, pp. 9–11) indicates that guilt may be a motive force in many cultures, Condit is wise in warning against unwarranted extrapolation of Western structures of thought to non-Western cultures. All of the scholars this study has noted as agreeing with Burke on the ontological nature of human guilt—Buber, Carroll, Heidegger, Reik—are in the Western, Judeo-Christian tradition, and the Judeo-Christian religion provides a rich literature in the symbolicity of guilt and redemption. More research into the importance of this motive structure in other cultures is warranted.

All of the above discussion of the ontological nature, or lack thereof, of guilt as a motivating force in discourse is presented in the interest of exploring the limits of the application of this theory. It should not obscure the fact that guilt need not be proven to be a universally dominant force, or even the dominant motive structure in America, for the guilt-purification-redemption cycle to be applicable to any particular discursive act. Even a cursory examination of the historical context (Burke's "scene") in which King's "I Have a Dream" speech took place would reveal that guilt over failure to live up to national principles was the essential motivating factor in overturning the system of segregation by race. To apply the guilt-purification-redemption model a critic does not need to accept Burke's claim as to the ontological nature of guilt, but only show that it was a motivating factor in the discourse under study.

Burke's theory of guilt, however, does not distinguish between collective guilt and individual guilt. A discursive form such as the guilt-purification-redemption drama that relies on a sense of collective responsibility for societal wrongs may not be fully effective in an individualistic society. That is probably why King's rhetoric of evoking then purifying white guilt appears more dated as the years go by. For post-civil-rights-era generations the link between America's past of slavery and overt segregation, and their present responsibility for those wrongs as manifested in support for affirmative action programs, is increasingly tenuous. For example, a recent poll found that 86 percent of whites, 76 percent of Latinos, and 60 percent of African Americans oppose using race as a factor in college admissions ("Prime Numbers," 2003).

MODES OF PURIFICATION

The existence of guilt, whether prelinguistic, linguistic, or arising out of a particular situation, requires purification. Purification is Burke's term for any means whereby guilt is transcended or removed. In Burke's theory, guilt, and thus the need for purification, is inherent in our nature. Burke maintains that although a scientific-rationalistic worldview attempts to deny this essentially moral-ethical aspect of our nature, it cannot be ignored. He asks not how forms of purification might be eliminated in a scientific culture, "but what new forms they take" (Burke, 1968b, p. 451; see also, Rueckert, 1982, pp. 46–47). In this section I will discuss what this book has contributed to our knowledge of the Burkean modes of purification, as well as consider what other modes of purification rhetorical critics should attempt to develop and apply.

This book has expanded our understanding of the Burkean modes of purification available to a rhetor. Burke usually cites victimage and mortification as the primary modes of purification, but this study demonstrates that purification through transcendence and through images of change, movement, and dramatic catharsis are also important modes of purification that need further study. Burke's emphasis on victimage and mortification has obscured our understanding of the multiplicity of ways in which purification may take place.

One of those ways, which I have chosen to keep in the victimage/mortification family because of its similarity to those forms, might be called purification through suffering, or by being a victim. Burke's emphasis on victimage as a scapegoating ritual for the purification of the guilt of those enacting the ritual, obscured to him the fact that scapegoating also purifies the scapegoat/victim. Burke (1973) says that in some circumstances the "*most perfect* sacrifice" [emphasis in original] is the person greatest in virtue; Christ being the archetypal example (p. 40). But Burke fails to note that by the same logic one may attain virtue by being a scapegoat or victim. Furthermore, Burke ignored the fact that once this form becomes self-reflexive (that is, once people can be shown that they are practicing or have practiced scapegoating), the guilt then turns back upon the perpetrator and the victim/scapegoat becomes purified not only in his or her own eyes (as one is when one knows one is being used as a scapegoat), but also in the eyes of society (as, for example, when a person is convicted of a crime and serves time for it, then it is later discovered that the person is innocent of the crime for which he or she was convicted). Also, Burke's emphasis on suffering through mortification (self-inflicted suffering) ignores the fact that suffering need not be self-inflicted to be purificatory—as a matter of fact, suffering at the hands of others is often more purificatory than mortification.

These other types of purification in the victimage/mortification family—purification through being a victim and purification through any type of suffering (whether inflicted deliberately by others, or as a result of one's social and economic circumstance, or even as the result of bad luck)—are today modes of purification with powerful appeal. Symbolizations of the suffering and victimization of oneself or one's group have probably always had strong rhetorical appeal, but are especially potent today in America (and throughout the world) because of social and cultural changes since World War II which have brought to our attention a history of unequal treatment and discrimination on the basis of gender, race, ethnicity, religion, and nationality. The Jewish Holocaust, American slavery, segregation, and oppression of African Americans, European colonization of African and Asian nations, and examples of unequal treatment of women, all provide rich veins of meaning for rhetors to draw upon in symbolizing victimization and suffering. Symbolization of the suffering and victimization of one's group has become such a powerful rhetorical form that a type of "oppression competition" has ensued in which groups compete in laying claim to greater degrees of past oppression. Power, as in the moral authority to be heard on certain issues and the right to receive preferential treatment in the allocation of society's resources (such as college admissions and employment hiring and promotion), is often allocated on the basis of the past record of victimization and suffering experienced by one's racial, ethnic, or sexual group.

This rhetoric of victimization has had important implications for political discourse and public policy. Symbolizations of victimage initially used to gain sympathy for a worthy cause and to motivate the community to effect healing and reconciliation—as in King's speech—often take on a power of their own that can have consequences beyond those initially intended. Edsall and Edsall's (1991) study demonstrates how, as the civil rights movement shifted from a focus on fundamental citizenship rights to a focus on equal outcomes achieved through racial preferences, black victimage became associated in the minds of many white Americans with special privileges in rights, employment, and education. A consequence of this has been that the core of the traditional Democratic Party constituency—the white working class, white ethnics, and white southerners—have come to regard themselves as victims of an alliance between the Democratic Party elite and special interest groups. These white voters frequently see their interests as separate from those of today's civil rights movement (pp. 3–31, 198–214). Further studies of the long-term effects of the rhetorical impact of symbolizations of victimage suffered by one's own racial, ethnic, sexual, or national group are warranted.

Another Burkean mode of purification this book has expanded upon is transcendence. Transcendence as a mode of purification has received little attention from rhetorical scholars. While Burke discusses transcendence fairly often in his writings, he provides little systematic treatment of it as a mode of purification, and among others, only Brummett (1981) has given transcendence any attention as a mode of purification. Burke emphasizes purification through rituals of victimage and scapegoating, which have their roots in primitive, religious practices. When updated to modern, mass societies, scapegoating often takes a sinister form, as in Hitler's scapegoating of Jews (see Burke, 1973, pp. 191–220) or southern segregationists' scapegoating of southern blacks. Burke's emphasis on this type of purification reflects his bias toward preindustrial rituals adapted to industrial-era societies of the mid-twentieth century. It may be that in postindustrial societies transcendence will prove a more potent form of purification. Transcendence may be a purificatory form adopted more by sophisticated and humane societies. Instead of dividing, it unites. Instead of emphasizing differences, it emphasizes similarities. It is no wonder then that in "I Have a Dream," King's paean to national unity and assimilation, his primary and most powerful mode of purification is transcendence (see chapter 4).

Purification through symbolizations of change, movement, and dramatic catharsis also has been little examined by rhetorical scholars. With the exception of dramatic catharsis, Burke mentions these processes more in passing than systematically. Rueckert (1982) pointed out the theme of movement and change in Burke's theory of purification (p. 104), and Hoban (1980) is the only rhetorical scholar I am aware of who has applied this theme critically. Purification through change, movement, and dramatic catharsis seems to operate at a more subtle, implicit level than the previously discussed forms. In King's speech we saw how the use of certain words, particularly metaphors, can subtly elicit images of change and movement. Also, we saw how change, movement, and dramatic catharsis is communicated in the overall structure of the speech, with its temporal progression from past promise, to present failure, to future realization of that promise, and the resolution of the conflict between good and evil for the soul of America (see chapter 4). Other studies could demonstrate the multiplicity of ways in which symbolizations of change, movement, transformations of various types (physical, social, psychological, spiritual), and dramatic catharsis could serve purificatory functions in rhetoric.

The modes of purification discussed in this study do not exhaust the modes of purification available. There are other modes of purification that rhetorical critics should study. The modes presented below are forms that do not, for the most part, fit neatly under any of the Burkean categories considered in this study. Although most of these are presented by the authors cited as purificatory actions (that is, nonlinguistic), they are all capable of being symbolized in discourse.

Jewett (1973) maintains that righteous violence can bring about redemption (pp. 177–214). Duncan (1962) says that comedy purges social guilt. He argues that the comic scapegoat becomes a sacrificial vessel through which we purge our projected social errors (as opposed to evils for the tragic scapegoat) and achieve social catharsis (pp. 395–402). (Although Duncan's way of putting it could be considered just a version of Burke's scapegoating, what about comedy in which there is no scapegoat? Does that not serve to reduce division and foster identification? Would that be considered a form of transcendence?) Carroll (1985) mentions a variety of ways in which guilt is dealt with, or "sublimated," to use his term. Guilt can be purged through the paying of reparations, taking the form of gift giving, the offering of praise, and of being especially nice to someone (pp. 17–18). Also, washing and cleaning oneself are ways of dealing with guilt. Carroll argues that in the West the modern soap and cosmetic industries exploit this socially prescribed ritual (p. 19). Carroll also mentions fasting, withdrawal into monasteries, and celibacy (forms of mortification), as well as "long and arduous pilgrimages to holy sites" (p. 19)—a combination of mortification and the journey, both of which are mentioned by Burke. Carroll cites chanting, singing, and praying as other means of sublimating guilt (are these forms of transcendence?). And finally, Carroll says that hard work is one of the most socially acceptable ways to sublimate guilt (p. 39). Solomon (1980) also notes the role of hard work in absolving guilt. She argues that the Right to Life movement "encourages individual supporters to purge their guilt through hard work for a good cause. The appeal is quite similar to the Christian notion of salvation through good works" (p. 61). This notion of purification through hard work warrants further study. It would seem that this is quite pervasive in social movements and political campaigns, and could be seen as a means of transcending the self for a larger cause. As far as I am aware, no systematic study has been done examining how participation itself in the civil rights movement might have proved a redemptive experience for participants.

It would behoove rhetorical scholars to come to a better understanding of the variety of means for purifying guilt and the implications of particular forms that purification can take. For example, might some forms be "better," (i.e., more humane, more effective) than others? Which forms would work best in which situations? What are the implications for the audience, or for the society in general, when guilt is purified through any particular mode? What would a study of the mode or modes of purification dominant in a particular culture tell us about that culture? (For that matter, what do the things people feel guilty about tell us about a particular culture, and what is the relationship between particular sources of guilt and the modes of purification used to absolve that guilt?)

GUILT-PURIFICATION-REDEMPTION AS A CULTURAL FORM

In Burke's theory one cannot escape guilt, and guilt implies the need for redemption through some process of purification. Therefore, the guilt-purification-redemption cycle is a form we are stuck with and the only issue is that of the forms that purification may take. However, in this section I want to move beyond the Burkean system and examine the implications of the redemption drama as a cultural form without assuming that the cycle must play itself out. In other words, what "trained incapacities" (Burke, 1984b, pp. 7–11) are induced by cultural adherence to this particular motive structure? By "trained incapacity" Burke means an orientation that causes one to act in a predetermined, but inappropriate way—a learned dysfunction. To see something in terms of "A" is to fail to see it in terms of "B" (see Burke, 1984b, pp. 7–11, 48–49). It is a type of conditioning or orientation that causes us to see something from a particular perspective to such a degree that we act out of that framework even when it does not fit the situation. For example, a struggling young businessperson may work long hours to provide financial security for his or her family, feeling that financial security is what the family needs to be happy. Then, long after financial security has been achieved, the businessperson continues to work long hours, because he or she is acting from an old perspective that no longer applies, failing to realize that what the family now needs is more time together as a family.

Guilt-purification-redemption is one such perspective or form for structuring and experiencing reality. Burke (1968a) defines form as "the creation of an appetite in the mind of the auditor, and the adequate satisfying of that appetite" (p. 31). Since form has to do with the "creation and gratification of needs," it "is 'correct' in so far as it gratifies the needs which it creates. The appeal of form in this sense is obvious: form *is* the appeal" [emphasis in original] (p. 138). Form provides "equipment for living" (Burke, 1973, pp. 293–304), in that the enactment of a form not only serves as a way of experiencing, but also creates incipient actions and attitudes that shape future action. This is so because words, and discourse in general, shape perspectives and serve as terministic screens for viewing the world (Burke, 1966, p. 44–47; 1968a, p. 143; Heath, 1989, p. 64). In sum, form is not incidental, but instrumental. Form is not merely the shape or structure the discourse happens to take, but it is the discourse as much as are the words, and it provides a pattern for viewing the situation and shaping future action. Thus, guilt-purification-redemption is a form in which the gratification of a felt need for redemption from guilt is satisfied through purification. This is not to say that because an orientation is adopted the form is always completed. Although the civil rights movement had many successes, in the movement as a whole the form of guilt-purification-redemption adopted by King and the moderate wing was never entirely completed. The movement splintered, black power advocates rejected the redemption framework (see chapter 7), and many whites, especially after the race riots of the middle and late sixties, abandoned the movement. Even in its particular manifestations the form did not always succeed. The campaign in Albany, Georgia, for example, failed to elicit white guilt, and sometimes demonstrations resulted in black violence, thus failing to elicit the sympathy needed for the redemption drama to succeed.

As a narrative form the guilt-purification-redemption cycle can be seen as a representative anecdote. A representative anecdote which is powerful in a particular culture provides a lens or template through which the critic can assess the values, concerns, and attitudes that culture brings to bear on issues for which that particular form is used. It tells the critic how the culture comes to terms symbolically with the issue. The articulation of a situation in discourse tells the audience how to deal with similar and related situations (see Brummett, 1984a, pp. 164, 166). Since a representative anecdote or form is obviously an orientation or perspective (a way of seeing the world) it can result in a trained incapacity. To see a situation as one requiring the purification of guilt is to fail to see other possibilities in the situation, to fail to see other ways of looking at it. Thus, to see events in the form of a redemption drama predetermines a certain range of actions and responses. If the need for the redemption of guilt is the lens through which we view a situation, then that viewpoint predetermines that the response will be the enactment of some mode or modes of purification.

In chapter 3 I argued that King's use of the theme of national redemption invoked a very potent myth, America's sense of itself as a special nation or chosen people with a God-given mission to redeem the world by making of itself a beacon of freedom, equality, and opportunity (see Jewett, 1973, p. 9; and Robertson, 1980, pp. 25–26, 122). This myth is doubly potent because it involves America's conception of its own founding and purpose as a secular New World in which the political ideas of the European Enlightenment could flourish and bear fruit, as well as the concept of America as a religious New World to which persecuted religious groups could come to freely practice their faith. A secularized redemption drama which retains its spiritual dimensions and suffuses the secular within the spiritual—as does the representative anecdote (underlying narrative form) in King's "Dream" speech—meets Burke's (1947) requirements for the "ideal myth," a vision which transcends the political, yet has political attitudes interwoven with it (p. 201). Any particular secular mythology by itself has an inherent weakness because it can always be "trumped" by a higher (sacred and absolute) standard. The power of King's rhetoric was in bringing that higher standard to bear on American secular mythology within the context of the civil rights movement. The guilt-purification-redemption drama is more than simply another narrative form. In America it is a powerful cultural form that combines our Judeo-Christian heritage with our European Enlightenment heritage.

What trained incapacities result from use of the guilt-purification-redemption form, especially in regard to the particular form of the secular/religious synthesis it takes in American public discourse? A full analysis in answer to that question is obviously beyond the scope of this book, but should prove a fruitful undertaking. Some learned dysfunctions in regard to the use of this form in dealing with the civil rights issue and race relations in general will be discussed in the next chapter, but for now I will venture some tentative observations on the learned dysfunctions of the redemption drama itself as a form for structuring and experiencing reality.

The first challenge in examining this form is simply in being able to step outside of it. If the initial premise of this form, that of the existence of guilt (whether prelinguistic, linguistic, or situational) is not accepted, then the form itself has no potency. However, a fairly strong case has already been made for the ontological nature of guilt, and at the least we have to admit that guilt occurs in certain situations. So the way to step outside of the form (the point of exit, so to speak) is not at the level of guilt, but at the next level, that of purification. Must guilt (again, speaking in the broad Burkean and Heideggerian sense) *always* require purification for the purpose of redemption? A guilt-purification-redemption form, especially one constructed in terms of ontological human guilt arising out of division, has the effect of construing divisions and differences as problems which much be overcome (purified), either through use of some transcendent, unifying terminology, or through some ritual of victimization in which a scapegoat is identified and symbolically destroyed or driven out. By seeing guilt (ontological human anxiety over our separation from one another) as something that must be overcome, this form ignores the possibility for a realistic acceptance of our state of separateness. Instead of accepting and resigning ourselves to perpetual division (anxiety) and accepting our differences from one another as inherent in our natures as individual monadic entities who can never achieve complete consubstantiality, we engage in a Sisyphean struggle to bridge the unbridgeable. The redemption drama may contribute to a trained incapacity toward trying to enact utopian visions of community instead of accepting a world of difference and imperfection.

If we look at guilt in Burkean terms (symbolically induced), as resulting from hierarchy, the "thou-shalt-nots," and failure to achieve perfection, we find the redemptive form drives us toward attempts to purify, to account for, these conditions. As we saw previously in this chapter, hierarchy is inevitable, and arises even in systems dominated by a discourse of equality. Should all hierarchies be considered bad? Also, should failure to achieve perfection, and violation of the rules of the social order, always require purification, or should they sometimes be accepted as part of our imperfect nature? Within a Burkean frame our ethical-moral natures cause us to be trapped in this recurring redemption cycle, but we can shape our own ethical-moral norms and decide upon the steps to be taken when those norms are violated. We do not have to be trapped in a guilt-purification-redemption form of experiencing and acting. Condit (1991) suggests that to move beyond this form we might look to the narrative forms of other cultures. For "non-victimage oriented forms, we might turn to the mythologic structure of Buddhism" (p. 5). Instead of being structured around the sin/redemption form, Buddhism, and other Eastern religions, such as Hinduism, are structured around an illusion/enlightenment form in which the individual strives to shed his or her illusions by seeing through the world of mere appearance to that of ultimate reality. (This is, of course, similar to Plato, but when Plato's ideas were Christianized, the movement from illusion to enlightenment became subsumed within the sin/redemption narrative. Enlightenment, insight into the mind of God, became one of the benefits of salvation by grace.) The West's economic and technological achievements could be seen in terms of sublimation of sin/guilt through hard work, while the East's illusion/enlightenment narrative has traditionally provided less incentive for worldly achievement. This is not to say that the East or West completely manifests these cultural forms in actual social praxis, but they do often function as ideal archetypes. Working within a cultural form in which the conditions of guilt require attempts at purification may cause us to be less accepting of differences, hierarchies, violations of social rules, and imperfection. The guilt-purification-redemption form can result in a trained incapacity toward seeing all manifestations of guilt (ontological anxiety, division, differences, disobedience to the social order) as problems which must be atoned for, instead of as normal conditions of human existence.

In a culture such as America, which has defined itself in terms of the assimilation of racial, ethnic, and religious groups under transcendent symbols—such as liberty, freedom, equality, justice, democracy—the redemption drama provides an ideal cultural form because of its emphasis on reducing division, differences, and hierarchy. But the costs may have been a failure to acknowledge our actual diversity. Furthermore, in America the redemptive cultural form has often resulted in zealous and unyielding attempts at national redemption through moralistic crusades (Morone, 2003). Rorabaugh (2002) states: "Throughout American history intensely hopeful periods such as the Progressive Era, the New Deal, and the sixties have invariably, if not inevitably, ended in disappointment, as reformers have discovered that the political, social, or cultural changes which they tried to make were far more difficult to accomplish than they had expected" (p. xii). Jewett also (1973) argues that these periods of great moral crusades with promises of national redemption are followed by periods of national disillusionment, of "long and counterproductive withdrawal[s]" when the promise is dashed (p. 49). For example, Jewett argues that after World War I and President Wilson's rhetoric about a "war to end all wars," Americans became disillusioned when the millennial peace did not follow. Thus, they were unable to deal with the complexities of a League of Nations to adjudicate further disputes. A rhetoric of unselfishness encourages "such illusions of moral superiority" that the people are often unable to deal with moral complexity (p. 50). Another example is the post-Reconstruction complacency toward the conditions of the former slaves after the zealous righteousness of the Abolitionist and Reconstruction periods. The pattern reemerged with the war on poverty and the civil rights movement (referred to by some as "the Second Reconstruction") of the 1960s, in which an initial period of idealistic moralism was followed by a period of disillusionment as the nation became more aware of the complexities of its social and racial problems (this point will be further developed in chapter 7). In short, the redemptive form has often been employed in America in a way that eschews the need for long-term consensus building and problem solving in favor of an absolutist and zealous rhetoric of redemption.

NOTE

1. I am indebted to Gregory Schufreider for his assistance with my interpretation of Heidegger's theory of guilt.

7

Evaluation of "I Have a Dream" and Its Legacy

In this chapter I will assess the effect and legacy of the "I Have a Dream" speech by answering the questions I posed in the preface, which are summarized as follows: (1) what myths and hierarchies does this speech invoke, and what conflicts does it transcend? (2) why did this speech emerge as the consensus voice on civil rights and what competing voices did it mute or ignore? (3) what are the limitations and contradictions of the message/form this speech employs? (4) what is the legacy of this speech? and (5) what are the consequences of a rhetoric of assimilation? Before answering those questions, however, it is necessary to briefly summarize what this book has argued concerning the significance of the "I Have a Dream" speech as a cultural icon, because the answers to the above questions depend upon recognition of the role this speech has taken on in American public discourse on race.

"I HAVE A DREAM" AS A CULTURAL ICON

I have argued that the representative anecdote (underlying narrative form) in King's "Dream" speech is a guilt-purification-redemption drama in which ontological human guilt, and white guilt over racism, is symbolically purged through: (1) victimage and mortification (or actually a form thereof in which black suffering under oppression performs a redemptive function); (2) transcendence; and (3) images of change, movement, and dramatic catharsis. I have further argued that the "I Have a Dream" speech can be seen as the representative anecdote (representative discursive act) of the moderate wing of the first phase of the civil rights movement and thus it functions as a text through which to examine the rhetorical appeals that proved so effective in overturning a decades-old system of legal segregation by race. But this speech is more than simply a representative text of the arguments of the moderate wing of the civil rights movement. This speech has taken on a powerful, symbolic role in American culture as an articulation of the vision of what the civil rights movement was striving for and as a national consensus of what America should be. More than any other individual, Martin Luther King, Jr., has come to symbolize for America the civil rights movement of the 1950s and 1960s (see, for example, Dyson, 2000, pp.7–8). While King is noted for many events and accomplishments—the Montgomery bus boycott, the Birmingham and Selma campaigns, the Nobel Peace Prize—it is through the "Dream" speech, with its repeated evocation in public discourse today of the symbol of "the dream" and the repeated playing of excerpts on television, that most Americans know of the ideas of Martin Luther King. When the speech is excerpted on television, usually the part of the speech excerpted is from the famous "dream" sequence. The phrase, "Martin Luther King's dream," or simply "the dream," is now a cultural ideograph that stands for the vision of an America of racial harmony and justice. Lentz (1990) wrote that "King's dream was of America made whole, and it was of such power that it fixed him as an inextirpable symbol in the culture" (p. 1). Tracy (1975) notes that certain historical personages can take on "symbolic dimensions," in that he or she becomes "representative of a certain human possibility for a particular cultural period" (p. 216). Tracy argues that Martin Luther King, especially after his death, took on such symbolic dimensions for many in American culture: "the culture's own memory-image of Martin Luther King became itself a cultural fact, a symbol, a representation of a particular authentic possibility" (p. 216). Thus, this speech is more than just another Burkean representative anecdote that provides a text through which to study a movement, and it is more than just the most famous speech of a famous American orator. King, and the speech, are contemporary cultural icons, symbols of the civil rights movement and the great American promise of freedom, justice, and equality.

THE MESSAGE/FORM OF THE "DREAM" SPEECH

This book set out to answer several questions concerning the rhetorical appeal of this speech, its impact on public discourse about race, and its legacy (see preface). The first question asked what is the message/form of this speech, what myths and hierarchies does the speech invoke, and what conflicts does it transcend? Chapters 2 through 5 have been an attempt to answer that question. We saw that the speech responded to a need on the part of Americans to have a sense that their guilt was purified—ontological human guilt, white guilt over racism and the failure of America to live up to her national ideals in regard to African Americans, and even black guilt resulting from low socioeconomic status and poor self-esteem after centuries of oppression. The speech drew upon, and merged, two primary myths: one secular, one religious, both powerful and central to America's conception of itself. The speech invoked America's dominant secular myth—that of itself as a special nation with a mission to provide freedom, justice, and opportunity to all people on an equal basis. This was merged by King (as it often is in American public discourse) with the dominant theme of the Judeo-Christian faith—that of the need for the redemption of sin (see Morone, 2003). By transcending the secular for the spiritual (that is, by placing the secular within the context of the spiritual), King was telling his auditors that by rising up to "live out the true meaning of its creed," America would not only achieve secular justice and national redemption for past failures, but that we as a people (and as individuals) would be spiritually redeemed because racial justice is in accord with the laws of God.

This allowed King to transcend the contradiction between white secular power and black moral and spiritual power. Duncan (1962) maintains that "Two social orders cannot exist side by side unless there are ways of translating one into the other, or unless one transcends the other" (p. 308). King's genius was to articulate a reconciliation in which white socioeconomic authority could be exchanged for black moral and spiritual authority. On a socioeconomic hierarchy, whites were superior to blacks, but because the civil rights movement was making white America aware of the history of oppression to which black Americans had been subjected, by 1963 blacks had developed superior moral and spiritual authority. King's rhetoric transcended the white social order of capitalism, materialism and competition for an order based on spiritual virtue, in which blacks were superior. He did this, however, by not totally rejecting the white value system, but by invoking its ultimate authority, God. Thus, for King, blacks had something to give whites in exchange for social and economic equality—i.e., the salvation of their souls and the reinvigoration of the national purpose.

THE CIVIL RIGHTS CONSENSUS VERSUS BLACK POWER

The second question I set out to answer was why the particular message/form of this speech emerged as the consensus voice on civil rights, and what competing voices were muted or ignored? To a large degree, the first part of this question was answered above and in the previous chapters: King's vision was articulate and inspiring, his persona appealing to moderate white America, and his message vividly exploited and merged America's most potent secular and religious myths. But to understand why King's vision became the consensus vision on civil rights we should place it in its historical and social context and assess the potency of the competing voices of the day.

Taylor (1985) analyzes the social upheavals of the 1960s as a national identity crisis in which America was in the process of exchanging one consensus for another. He argues that before the 1960s the U.S. consensus had been that of a society of production, and people in the mainstream took their role therein. By the 1960s, however, the national infrastructure had been built and America was relatively affluent (although, as we discovered, that affluence was not evenly distributed). By 1963 America had achieved unmatched economic and military supremacy. Therefore, by the 1960s economic production and growth was no longer the overriding national concern, but there was no national identity with which to replace the production ethos. The youth rebellion of the sixties (of which the civil rights movement was the vanguard) came from a search for a new identity to replace the old consensus (Taylor, 1985, pp. 48–51). This vacuum—in an environment of postwar national affluence and international dominance, along with the coming of age of the baby boom generation fed on the idealism of this postwar national affluence—allowed a social reform consensus to emerge to replace the production ethos (see Rorabaugh, 2002).

African Americans, on the margins of the old consensus and with their growing sense of purpose and unity from the civil rights movement, were in a position to play a leading role in defining and shaping the new consensus, and to redefine their relationship to the mainstream. In a social reform paradigm, their historical role as oppressed victims gave them superior moral authority in the new emerging consensus. King's rhetoric articulated the new relationship of black America to mainstream America. Blacks were America's redeemers. A new set of cultural practices, a reinterpretation of America's mission was in the process of being articulated. Thus, America made a tremendous investment in social reform (LBJ's "Great Society") to redeem itself from social injustice. The new identity for America, the new moral crusade, was social justice and equality. King's dream was the most succinct and vivid articulation of that new vision. To convict America of a moral failure of social justice in allocating its wealth, the natural paradigm to draw upon was the Christian redemption drama merged with the promise of secular, national redemption. King's speech came at a propitious time to serve the purpose of galvanizing a new national consensus. The speech occurred late enough in American history that it could be seen live by millions on television and recorded for posterity, and yet early enough that America had not yet lost its sense of national purpose and conviction. In the wake of Vietnam, the social upheavals and changes of the late 1960s, and then the Watergate scandal, it is doubtful that America could again coalesce around a vision based upon secular national redemption and Christian mythology. In invoking King's vision today, we are squeezing life out of a vision based upon myths that no longer have the same valence in our culture, but for which we have yet to find a replacement.

The emerging consensus, however, was not embraced by everyone. To determine which voices King's dream muted or ignored it is useful to look for those voices that criticized King's vision. Of course, King's dream was not shared by segregationists, but their harsh rhetoric and sometimes violent tactics, along with the increasingly obvious contradiction between America's principles of justice and the oppressive practice of segregation, made this a growingly untenable position to hold. However, King's speech received criticism from another quarter as well. While the term "black power" did not enter into public discourse until 1966, the forerunners of the black power movement, in the persons of Malcolm X and the increasingly radical young activists at SNCC and CORE, were not entirely pleased with King's speech and the reaction it received. Malcolm X (1965) criticized King and the other march organizers for "selling out" to the white power structure (pp. 13–17). Hare (1965) said the speech "was but a reaffirmation of [King's] faith in the white power structure" and noted that it "led Malcolm X to point out that while King is dreaming, other Negroes are having nightmares" (p. 40). Marable (1984) writes: "Militants were bitterly disappointed that King had chosen not to include extensive critical remarks on the recent racist violence in the South, and the failure of most white liberals to respond concretely to the Negro's economic plight" (p. 82). As the black power movement began to coalesce around 1965–66 it found its voice muted by the assimilationist vision King had articulated so effectively at the March on Washington. The American media had come to feel it had an "investment" in Martin Luther King since they had christened him as the voice of reason and moderation in the civil rights movement (see Lentz, 1990). There is a long tradition in American public discourse on race, established at the time of Booker T. Washington, of asking, "Who speaks for the Negro?" The press was accustomed to seeking out the single black leader who was supposed to be the spokesperson for all of black America. Thus, when black power advocates criticized King's position on civil rights, they were marginalized and presented by the media as unrepresentative, violence-prone radicals.

Black power advocates rejected King's assimilationist vision and turned instead to a model emphasizing black self-respect and stressing the importance of blacks taking control of their own institutions of economic and political empowerment. Generally, black power advocates rejected the assimilationist vision because after 1965 they began to feel that it was not working and/or because they felt the assimilationist model required blacks to sacrifice their culture in order to blend into the dominant white society. "Black power" was a 1960s slogan which resurrected a long tradition—from the slave rebellions of Nat Turner and others, to the protests of Frederick Douglass, to the black nationalism of Marcus Garvey—of blacks taking the responsibility for the emancipation and development of their race into their own hands (see Barbour, 1968, pp. 17–58; and Colston, 1979, pp. 233–235). Even Booker T. Washington, who is normally seen as an accommodationist to the white power structure of his day, can be seen in this tradition because of his emphasis on black economic self-reliance, self-pride, self-segregation, and racial cohesion (see Colston, 1979, p. 234; and Newman, 1987, pp. 65–72).

Space does not permit, nor does my purpose call for, a thorough explication of the philosophy of black power, or a discussion of every strand of the movement and every statement made in its name. Some black power elements did advocate aggressive violence against whites, but that was rarely put into practice and most responsible black power spokespersons insisted only upon the right of blacks to use violence in self-defense or as the only means to free themselves from oppression when all other avenues had been exhausted (in contrast to King's admonitions that blacks should not use violence under any circumstances, even in self-defense). While some black power advocates did speak of "black nationalism" in literal terms—that is, of the formation of a separate black nation in America or Africa—most considered that unrealistic and saw black nationalism in terms of "self-consciousness and group-identity . . . or the conviction that participation in one community is not incompatible with ties of sentiment and support for another community where one has ethnic loyalties" (Newman, 1987, p. 28). Even Martin Luther King, late in his career, began incorporating into his philosophy of love and nonviolence the need for black self-respect and the establishment of black economic and political power bases (see M. L. King, 1986, pp. 245–252; Scott, 1968). However, as Lentz (1990) and Dyson (2000) have demonstrated, King's increasing radicalism was muted by the American media who did not want to abandon their investment in King as the chief voice of moderation, reasonableness, and nonviolence in the civil rights struggle. Thus, and especially so after his death and martyrdom in 1968, King was presented by the American media as the articulator of "the dream" and the symbol of the integrationist consensus which developed on civil rights, and which was consistent with America's "melting pot" theory of ethnic assimilation. In contrast, the American media focused upon the most radical elements of the black power movement (in part because they made better copy than did its moderate spokespersons), so that the whole movement was seen as racist, antiwhite, separatist, and in general, a direct threat to America's assimilationist vision of itself. In America the assimilationist vision—and its 1960s manifestation in the integrationist consensus (King's "dream")—has so dominated our discourse and thinking on racial and ethnic issues that it is difficult to stand outside of it to find a position from which to critique it. The assimilationist vision has become a defining feature of American national identity and of the individual identity of most Americans. The ideas of the more moderate wing of the black power movement allow a critique of, and alternative to, King's integrationist vision as articulated in the "Dream" speech.[1]

Black power advocates, more directly and forcefully than integrationists, acknowledged two conditions concerning race relations in America. First, they recognized white America's deep-seated and long-abiding racism, and the difficulty of removing that racism (and acceptance that it may never be removed). Newman (1987) wrote that the "presupposition [of black power is] that the assimilationist-accommodationist position is made untenable by the conscious and unconscious racism of white America, an aspect of culture so deep, strong and widespread that it can never be eliminated (p. 27). Lester (1966) argued that blacks had been "naive" and "idealistic" in buying into "the American lie of assimilation," and that it was now time for blacks to focus on their own identity and seek control of their own institutions (pp. 22, 24–25). Secondly, black power advocates more openly acknowledged the long-term effects of racism on an oppressed minority. Racism had left African Americans with low self-esteem and inferior socioeconomic status, and thus at a power disadvantage in dealing with whites. Therefore, black power spokespersons argued, the assimilationist model put blacks in the position of supplicants seeking admission into the majority culture on the terms of that majority culture. Poussaint (1968) wrote: "Assimilation by definition always takes place according to the larger societal (white) model of culture and behavior, and thus the Negro must give up much of his black identity and subculture to be comfortably integrated" (p. 99). Wright (1968) maintained that the integrationist approach had failed: "There can be no meaningful integration between unequals. Thus as black men have turned toward an illusive integrationist goal, with white men holding the reins of power, black men have lost both their identity and their self-respect" (p. 116).

Black power advocates, then, turned toward a more pluralistic model of American society, stressing the need to build black self-respect and institutions of black empowerment in order to be able to approach white America from a position of mutual respect and equality. Hare (1965) said blacks should reject the assimilationist approach because it requires the adopting of white standards and norms, and it "undermines" black "self-respect and self-sufficiency" (pp. 172–173). He argued that blacks should instead adopt a "pluralistic approach," like the Jews and French Canadians, who demand "equality of opportunity and equality of citizenship," but also seek to "preserve group identity as a distinct ethnic group" (p. 174). Carmichael (1966) argued that the approach that called for integrating blacks into the mainstream of American society was "based on the assumption that there was nothing of value in the Negro community" (p. 645). The integrationist model, he maintained, by appealing to the conscience and goodwill of white society, left blacks in a position of dependence (pp. 646–647). Even a group as respectable as the National Committee of Negro Churchmen endorsed a version of black power. In a statement on black power they called for:

> A more equal sharing of power . . . as the precondition of authentic human interaction. . . . Without this capacity to *participate with power*—that is, to have some organized political and economic strength to really influence people with whom one interacts—integration is not meaningful. [emphasis in original] ("Black Power," 1968, p. 267)

Because of the unequal distribution of power, and the sense on the part of much of white America that blacks had nothing of value to offer, integration became "irrelevant" to many black power advocates (Lester, 1966, p. 25; Newman, 1987, p. 10). They turned instead to a philosophy that stressed building black self-respect, discovering and appreciating black cultural identity, and establishing institutional bases of economic and political power in the black community. As one black power spokesperson put it at an Atlanta forum: "Martin King was trying to get us to love white folks before we learned to love ourselves, and that ain't no good" (cited in Harding, 1968, p. 4). Harding (1968) argued that before black Americans could fully participate in and identify with a larger community (whether that be the American community or humankind at large), they had to develop a healthy self-esteem and identification with their own racial and cultural heritage (pp. 5–11). Thus, a "temporary withdrawing of the black community into itself" was necessary to strengthen the black community and prepare it for true interdependence with white America on a basis of mutual respect and true equality (p. 20).

In sum, black power advocates were not optimistic about the chances of achieving true integration, at least in the short run, because they did not expect white America to voluntarily cede its power advantage in anything more than a token and piecemeal fashion, and they did not believe that *true* integration and equality could occur between races in a situation where power is unequally distributed. King's integrationist approach assumed blacks would attain power *as a result* of being fully integrated into American society, whereas black power advocates believed that power is a *prerequisite* to true integration. King's integrationist vision came to dominate public discourse on civil rights, marginalizing and muting the philosophy of black power, and depriving the assimilationist model of the healthy criticism it needed to adapt and maintain viability. Harding (1968) criticized King for his failure to offer anything more, in the face of white intransigence, than vague statements of "faith" that justice will eventually triumph: "King stands for the liberal tradition, continuing to maintain faith in American goodness, in reason, in the ordered nature of the world." King "substitutes an eloquent dream" for a realistic appraisal of America's racist nature (pp. 34–35). However, the black power advocates, according to Harding, sometimes went too far in stressing the forces of evil in society, refusing "to dream" or sufficiently acknowledge the possibility of creative healing (pp. 35–36). Harding expressed the need for a perspective that balances the two approaches by combining black power's willingness to look realistically upon the evil of American racism with King's recognition of the possibility for healing and his "determination not to succumb to the enemy's disease" (p. 36).

The black power perspective offers a ground from which to critique King's assimilationist vision. His emphasis on love, nonviolence, and moral persuasion leaves the oppressed minority in a position of dependence on the goodwill of the majority and without effective compensatory power if and when that goodwill wanes. His "Dream" speech fails to fully acknowledge the depth of American racism and the difficulty of overcoming it and achieving true integration. King's vision also fails to appreciate the argument of the black power advocates that a race that has been brutally and systematically oppressed cannot step immediately into a position of integration into the majority culture without losing its ethnic identity. *True* equality requires *inter*dependence and *mutual* respect. Therefore, the argument goes, a period of black self-nurturing, self-empowerment, and community-building may be necessary before blacks can approach whites as true equals who have as much to offer as they expect to receive in return. Also, King tended to conflate equality with integration. He failed to realize what black power advocates realized full well; that integration *does not* necessarily mean that one is integrated on an *equal* basis. Nor did he seem to recognize the possibility of a pluralistic approach in which equality does not necessarily *require* integration. King's tendency to translate *political* problems into *moral* issues, as Gandhi had in India, created a sense of separation between power and moral authority which made power seem "bad" to him and his followers.

THE SHORTCOMINGS OF THIS MESSAGE/FORM

The third question I set out to answer in this book concerns the shortcomings of the particular message/form King chose to employ in his speech at the

March on Washington. In other words, what are its limitations and contradictions? What thought patterns does it encourage and discourage? What learned dysfunctions does it produce?

The rhetorical form of redemption from guilt that marked King's "I Have a Dream" speech is the paradigm for the moderate wing of the civil rights movement. Steele (1990) believes "that in the sixties the need for white redemption from racial guilt became the most powerful, yet unspoken, element in America's social-policy-making process" (p. 79). The problem with the guilt paradigm, which conceives of America's racial problems in terms of white guilt and black victimage, is that achieving the moral high ground in terms of the cleansing of sin for whites and maintenance of innocence for blacks counts more than achieving actual results. Steele (1990) has commented upon the two major elements of the guilt paradigm: white guilt and black victimage. He argues that the need for white redemption shaped the nation's policies regarding blacks in ways that delivered the look of innocence without doing much to uplift blacks (pp. 79–80). He further states that guilt can be a "very dangerous" motive because it has a tendency "to draw us into self-preoccupation and escapism" in which we are no longer interested in the source of our guilt and an authentic redemption from it, but only the *look* and *appearance* of redemption (pp. 84–85). Thus, the paradigm of white guilt makes the real problems of blacks secondary (for whites) to the preoccupation of whites with the need for quick redemption (Steele, 1990, pp. 87–88). One result of the need for white redemption was the enactment of affirmative action programs. However, these programs were not established through broad public support, but through executive orders, Equal Employment Opportunity Commission guidelines, and the courts. Thus, they were often seen as a punishment handed down from above, creating resentment and causing the programs to lack legitimacy among many whites. Nieli (1991) argues that white guilt over past racial sins of the white race resulted in a fear of opposing preferential treatment for blacks, even though racial preferences and distinctions violate a central principle of the early civil rights movement—that race should not be a factor in the awarding of benefits. Thus, the use of the guilt paradigm in arguing for racial equality contained within it the seeds of a policy that contradicted the original goals of the movement.

The other side of the coin of white guilt is black victimage. For whites to be guilty, blacks must be victims. Steele (1990) argues that being black has come to be identified with being a victim (p. 107). Victimization carries with it a certain authority and power, but the power of victimage can be a dangerous power for two reasons. First, while victimage spares one from some degree of guilt and responsibility, one must maintain the state of victimage to maintain one's innocence. Steele makes this point when he argues that the tragedy of black power today is that it is primarily a "victim's power"—a power rooted "too deeply in the entitlements derived from past injustice." This formula "binds the victim to his victimization by linking his power to his status as a victim" (p. 14). Second, the power of victimage is a passive power that depends upon the elicitation of guilt in the conscience of the victimizer. In this formula, the victimizer is the active agent of change, while the victimized is a mere passive receiver. The analysis of the "second persona" in chapter 5 has already demonstrated how King's metaphors cast the audience in a passive role. Steele (1990) notes that since social victims have been oppressed by society, they come to feel that their lives will be improved more by change in society than by individual action. Society rather than self becomes the agent of change and individual passivity is encouraged (pp. 14–15). In 1966 the National Committee of Negro Churchmen warned of the consequences of this "distortion" and "gross imbalance of power and conscience between Negroes and white Americans." While it is assumed

> that white people are justified in getting what they want through the use of power . . . Negro Americans must . . . make their appeal only through conscience. As a result, the power of white men and the conscience of black men have both been corrupted. The power of white men is corrupted because it meets little meaningful resistance from Negroes to temper it. . . . The conscience of black men is corrupted because, having no power to implement the demands of conscience, the concern for justice is transmuted into a distorted form of love, which, in the absence of justice, becomes chaotic self-surrender. Powerlessness breeds a race of beggars. ("Black Power," 1968, p. 264)

In sum, a certain irony results when the guilt paradigm is used by a historically oppressed group to achieve power. First, the oppressors, convicted of their guilt, become more interested in receiving absolution for their sins than in changing the conditions of oppression. Of course, changing conditions of oppression is one way to bring about absolution, but changing conditions of oppression is only secondary to the goal of absolution. For those convicted of social and moral failings, the primary concern is to achieve the appearance of redemption in as quick and painless a manner as possible. The second irony of the guilt paradigm is that it links the power of the oppressed to their status as oppressed. Thus, victims develop a stake in maintaining their status as victims, a status which places them in a condition of passivity and dependability. King's discourse failed to make a distinction between blacks as victims in a moral/spiritual order and blacks as victims in a sociopolitical sense (in fact, he merges these two orders of experience). When moral/spiritual victimage, for which one must rely upon the ultimate judgment of God, subsumes sociopolitical victimage, the victim is encouraged to passivity in the sociopolitical realm.

Of course, in King's use of the guilt paradigm African Americans' role as victims was subsumed under a transcendent vision of national unity and secular/spiritual redemption. But the guilt paradigm itself, especially when the social values and myths upon which transcendence depends begin to fray, lends itself to a rhetoric of victimization. King's discourse established a powerful rhetorical form for dealing with race relations in America, which for later, lesser rhetors has often deteriorated into a rhetoric of victimization. In the hands of a rhetor less ethical than Martin Luther King a redemption drama can become an insidious and divisive paradigm in which one party has an excessive stake in convicting the other of guilt in order to insure and maintain the first party's innocence and power as a victim. Loury (1989) argues that many black leaders have come to base black claims:

> [A]bove all, on the status of blacks as America's historical victims. Maintenance of this status requires constant emphasis on the wrongs of the past and exaggeration of present tribulations. He who leads a group of historical victims . . . must renew the indictment and keep alive the moral asymmetry implicit in the respective positions of victim and victimizer. . . . The circumstance of his group as "underdog" becomes his most valuable political (and cultural) asset. (p. 147)

Sleeper (1990) has demonstrated how this process played out in New York City. His study describes how the racial politics of guilt and redemption has been used by racial demagogues such as Al Sharpton to achieve personal power through exploiting racial divisiveness, led to excesses such as the Tawana Brawley affair, and resulted in alienation and mistrust between the races. Williamson (2002) sees the rhetoric of redemption as a powerful cultural form that can help us overcome a history of racism and bigotry, but a form that can also oversimplify the complexity of race relations. The redemption drama "acts as a sort of moral *reductio ad absurdum*. We are encouraged by its perfection to see it as a metonymy for all of our racial problems" (p. 255).

THE LEGACY OF "I HAVE A DREAM"

Next, this book set out to ascertain the legacy of King's speech. To what degree did the success of this speech's message/form contribute to the civil rights movement's failure to achieve its goals beyond the dismantling of legal segregation?

"I Have a Dream" is the paradigmatic example of, and indeed helped to establish, the moral/religious approach adopted by most mainstream civil rights advocates. The legacy of this speech is in the way its particular message/form was elevated as the "correct" prism through which to view the civil rights issue, to the point that its assumptions and goals became unquestioned aspects of public culture; indeed it became almost a sacred text. Duncan (1968) has noted the tendency for articulations of ideal futures to become sacrosanct: "Once the promise is symbolized and these symbols become sacred, they are no longer subject to critical discussion" (p. 113). This is what happened with the "Dream" speech, as the martyred hero and his "dream" became the centerpiece of a symbolic cluster representing what the nation told itself was a commitment to racial justice. To question the heroism of King, or the desirability of achieving "the dream," was to risk having hurled upon one the culture's most venomous epithet—"racist."

But a movement based on moral and religious arguments can often get bogged down in zealous moralism, self-righteousness, religious mythology, and spiritual otherworldliness. Andrew A. King (1971), in his study of the rhetorical legacy of the black church, found that because of their religious roots, civil rights spokespersons tended to see the movement in terms of biblical typology and religious mythology, resulting in a rhetoric that "rendered its goals impressionistic and illusory" (p. 183). Martin Luther King was the exemplar of this approach with his focus upon the black man, made morally righteous through his suffering, as the redeemer of America. King's rhetoric encouraged whites and blacks to "act out the old Biblical romance of oppressors versus chosen people" (A. A. King, 1971, p. 184). Marable (1985) places King within the "Black Moses" tradition of black American politics in which an individual arises to challenge the racist system and inspire a "new vision of social relations. The political discourse is almost always connected with the Old Testament saga of Moses" (p. 304). The weakness of this paradigm, according to Marable, is that one individual becomes the conduit of black social revolt and people fail to see that the power to act is in their own hands (p. 305).

Some have argued that the religious approach to civil rights only prolongs oppression by deflecting the need for sociopolitical action in the here and now. Hernton (1966) criticizes "mystical" solutions calling for "love," "suffering," and "forgiveness," employing such phrases as "Go down Moses," and "I Have a Dream," and telling black people that God is on their side. Such approaches tend "to transport the Negro's concentration *away* from *this* world and *this* time, a world and time that, if he is to become free, he must deal with in an objective, secular fashion" [all emphases in original] (p. 80). Andrew A. King (1971) argues that "to achieve secular equality, it is necessary to appeal to audiences in terms of realistic alternatives; the supplication of supernatural powers only deflects action" (p. 185).

King's use in "I Have a Dream" of transcendent images and his synthesis of religious/secular mythology gave America a legacy of dealing with its racial problems in terms of abstraction and myth. In order to prove devotion to the ideals of racial justice, white Americans simply had to declare allegiance to the proper symbols and myths. Burke (1973) wrote, "The reading of a book on attaining success is in itself the symbolic attaining of that success" (p. 299). The same could be said of listening to, or reading, or repeating the language of a speech, especially once those words have become transfixed in the national consciousness as secular ideals. The invocation and repetition of King's words and ideas allow Americans to *symbolically* attain racial justice. We attain racial justice—purge ourselves of guilt, prove our worthiness to be included in the community of right-thinking, racially enlightened people—by our acceptance of the symbols of racial justice. What we want is easy redemption, and we get it in symbolic form.

Kendall (1965) predicted that the civil rights movement would ultimately fail to substantially alter the lives of the majority of the black masses because it had not achieved a true *political* consensus for the type of change it was seeking. There is a danger in achieving a moral consensus without achieving a true political consensus to go along with it—that is, without having achieved political consensus on the sacrifices involved and the means necessary to realize the new moral vision. King's speech gave America an inspiring vision of a new moral order, but it elided the costs and difficulties of achieving racial equality. King cannot be held entirely responsible for the legacy of his speech, or the way Americans have chosen to use his words. King was a preacher who felt his job was to inspire people and give them a better vision of themselves. His "Dream" speech, although idealistic and unrealistic, did that. But America has used the speech as a national mantra. The mere invocation of the words and ideas provide us with symbolic purification and transcendence for our failure to achieve racial harmony.

CONSEQUENCES OF A RHETORIC OF ASSIMILATION

The final question this book sought to answer was: What are the consequences of a successful, totalizing rhetoric of assimilation? Does the need to transcend differences necessarily result in a discourse which elides the practical difficulties of achieving assimilation? Can real, long-term divisions be transcended without ignoring the sociopolitical difficulties of effecting such assimilation?

We saw that in the case of the "I Have a Dream" speech the difficulties of achieving integration are elided in favor of an emphasis on inspiration toward the goal itself. Although the speech has been widely praised (see chapter 3), some have criticized the speech as being empty of substance. Lewis

(1978) said the speech "was rhetoric almost without content" (p. 228). One observer, a young, radical black, admitted that he and his friends got caught up in the moment, but upon reflection found the speech lacking: "we were screaming and yelling and wah-hooing, but after it was over, I said to myself, 'What did he say?'" ("The March of Time," 1973, p. 26). Terrell (1989) contended that in contrast to John Lewis's censored speech that was "dangerously relevant," King's speech "wasn't censored because it was basically irrelevant. . . . About the best thing that can be said for King's speech is that it proved beyond a doubt that he was a truly great orator who had pleasant dreams" (p. 985).

It is perhaps unfair to fault King himself for the fact that his speech contained little substantive analysis of the difficult racial problems confronting America. King was a preacher and that day he preached (for analyses of King's preaching, see Lischer, 1995; and Warren, 2001). King's oratorical genius was in his ability to apply America's religious/moral values to secular issues in a visionary way. "I Have a Dream" was a secular sermon addressed to the nation, and it did what any good Sunday church sermon does. A religious sermon inspires the listeners to seek the Kingdom of God, and King's speech inspired the nation to seek a secular Kingdom of God in race relations. King was not a nuts-and-bolts leader who excelled in details. He was a national moral leader who provided vision and inspiration. As this book has demonstrated, "I Have a Dream" is best understood as a national, secular version of a Christian redemption drama.

Americans misuse the speech when they try to treat it as anything more than an inspirational sermon (albeit a great one) articulating an ideal vision. Alvarez (1988) argues that King's "I Have a Dream" is best understood as a sermon in the black Baptist tradition employing dialogic form, repetition, rhythm, and the use of common knowledge. Marbury (1989) says that King's rhetoric was in the style of biblical rhetoric—a preliterate, oral style in which the rhetor is caught up in the power of the revealed word of God. "I Have a Dream"—especially in the second half of the speech with its repetition, rhythm, vivid imagery, and use of mythos—is rhetoric in the oral, pre-literate mode, similar to the Homeric style of rhetoric identified by Havelock (1963, pp. 3–193). The "dream" sequence—the most stirring, the most memorable part of the speech—does not move one nearly as much in the reading as in the hearing, unless one reads the text mentally employing King's famous cadence and rhythm (as a matter of fact, it is difficult to read those words without mentally employing King's cadence because the words and the cadence are so intricately interwoven in our minds). As Havelock observed about the Homeric rhetoric, oral rhetoric derives its effect from its participative and rhythmic nature. In order to analyze the content we must step back, as Plato did with the work of the poetic bards of Greece, and say, "What does this mean?" that is, examine it objectively. In order to examine the content of King's message we must arouse our consciousness from its dreamlike state induced by the language and rhythm to stimulate our minds to think conceptually about what is being said. King's speech provides vivid images of freedom, justice, and equality in the "dream" sequence, but this is embedded in the narrative form. There are no articulations of "freedom" or "justice" as concepts that then can be applied outside the context of King's narrative. Thus, the "Dream" speech is confined to a role as an inspirational vision or goal, but serves no function as a road map of how to get there. It provides few concepts or definitions that can be carried over to apply to various situations. The "dream" is invoked as a goal, as identification, as the sharing of a vision of racial harmony and justice, but it provides no more than that.

A discourse employing a totalizing rhetoric of assimilation, by necessity, elides the practical difficulties of achieving that assimilation. Although later in his career King was more realistic in regard to the difficulties of achieving true racial harmony and integration (see Dyson, 2000, pp. 31–35, 39–40), "I Have a Dream" articulates the promise of an unrealistic utopia. Walton's (1971) study of King's political philosophy concludes that King unrealistically attempts to impose a religious ethic of "pure love" (or, as King called it "agape") into the secular realm where justice can only be partial and temporary at best. King's philosophy ignores "man's egoism and self-interest" which tend to "render all historical harmonies of interest partial and incomplete" (p. 80). Walton argues that King's attempt to forge high religious idealism with a practical methodology

> [R]esulted in an insistence on the coming into being of a purely utopian community, a just society which, if it ever were to be attained, would require a much greater transformation than any ever envisioned by King. The gap between the ideal envisaged and the reality at hand is much too ponderous to be bridged by powerful convictions. (p. 100)

Walton concludes that King made an error common to political theologians in his attempt to convert moral values based on divine revelation and belief in God into a political ideology applicable "to all people in all situations." King's thought is "most directly applicable in those religious communities with a common background to his own," and is increasingly less relevant as one moves away from such communities (p. 116). King's greatest success came as a leader of the church-based civil rights movement in the South, but when King attempted to expand his movement to the northern cities, his message was less relevant and his campaigns were less successful. It may be that King's focus on changing political institutions rather than cultural institutions constricted the potential success of his message. His partial successes were implemented by Congress and the courts, but these political authorities can only craft and enforce regulations, they do not create opportunity. Most activities that foster organic attitudinal change and create opportunities go on outside of government, in business and cultural institutions.

King's philosophy was based on faith in God and belief in the power of redemptive love to transform the hearts of human beings, but King's political and legal successes were not a result of changing hearts and minds through the power of redemptive love. Ultimately all of his successes came about as the result of economic boycotts, court rulings, or from generating sympathy and embarrassment by inducing segregationists to violent overreaction. For King the ultimate goal of the movement was love and reconciliation between the races. But it is not necessary for blacks and whites to "love" each other in order to attain racial justice and equality. What is necessary is that race not be a factor in civil, legal, and economic matters.

Instead of confronting the harsh realities of America's racial problems and allowing for human imperfection in implementing solutions, King's assimilationist vision viewed race relations in terms of a socioreligious mythic drama. Walton (1971) notes that projecting reality into mythic drama is essential for moving the imagination of people, but there can be profound and long-lasting consequences from the adoption of appealing social myths. Even though their ideals may not be attainable, they can shape thought and behavior for long periods of time (p. 88). A successful discourse of totalizing, assimilationist rhetoric can, as in the case of King's "Dream" speech, create and reinforce social myths that are harmful in their failure to acknowledge human imperfectability and the trade-offs always necessary to forge any degree of social cohesion. This is both the power and weakness of assimilating mythologies. They bring us together, but by eliding our differences. King's views were simplistic in their two-valued view of the world. Dualities such as good versus evil, justice versus injustice, nonviolence versus violence, and so on, ignore the fact that human nature and human institutions are both good and bad, just and unjust, and that any system which implements a measure of justice requires some degree of coercion. Reik (1957) argues that the danger in seeking moral perfectability is in overreaching (p. 424). In an ardent quest for virtue human beings often institute a reign of terror, as in the French Revolution, in an attempt to enforce virtue and justice. Reik recommends that we give up ideas of our own "grandiosity and perfectability" and not make exaggerated moral demands upon ourselves (p. 428). Attempts to implement King's assimilationist vision of perfect equality and justice are vulnerable to this danger. Duncan (1962) notes that there is always a danger in "equality" being used as a slogan to mask or promote one particular type of hierarchy over another (p. 338).

King's envisioned utopia would not be a world in which inequality (or hierarchy) is really eliminated, but one that inverts the present hierarchy based on economic and political power for one based on some people's conception of spiritual goodness and moral virtue.

A successful transcendent vision tautologically elides social division. An alternative to dealing with race relations through the prism of assimilationist utopianism and socioreligious mythology is the approach of the black power advocates discussed earlier in this chapter. The black power approach avoided the unrealistic utopianism of King's vision that came to dominate our discourse on civil rights. King's assimilationist model would have been well served by incorporating a critique from the black power perspective. However, a weakness of the pluralistic, black power perspective is that it does not transcend our differences. This is why it was largely rejected by America (although some elements of it have been incorporated into our approach to race relations). At the beginning of this section I asked whether there are means whereby a rhetor can transcend real, bitter, long-term divisions of race, class, religion, and so on, under a higher good without ignoring the sociopolitical difficulties of effecting such an assimilation. I have concluded that King's assimilationist model transcended divisions, but at the expense of a realistic assessment of the sociopolitical difficulties of effecting that assimilation. The black power advocates acknowledged the difficulties of overcoming these divisions, but provided no transcending vision of unification.

THE COMIC FRAME

It is difficult to imagine an approach to the civil rights debate of the 1960s that would have avoided the shortcomings of the two alternatives discussed above. In an effort to outline a perspective that might have provided an alternative to the Scylla of King's vision of redemptive assimilation and the Charybdis of division and bitterness in the black power perspective, this chapter will conclude with a brief explanation of Burke's (1984a) concept of "the comic frame" (pp. 39–44, 166–175). The comic frame has been little studied by rhetorical scholars (the exceptions are Carlson, 1986, 1988; and Crusius, 1999, pp. 202–208), so this treatment is meant merely to suggest what an alternative view on American race relations in the 1960s might have looked like; a view which avoids the shortcomings of King's redemptive mythology, but which also avoids the divisiveness of the black power approach.

Burke (1984a) argues that our "structures of symbolism" might be understood through the terminology of literary forms, and that each form "stresses its own peculiar way of building the mental equipment (meanings, attitudes, character) by which one handles the significant factors of his time" (p. 34). In other words, literary forms can be seen as "frames of acceptance" or "strategies for living" (p. 43). The comic frame, according to Burke (1984a), "should enable people *to be observers of themselves, while acting*. Its ultimate would not be *passiveness*, but *maximum consciousness*. One would 'transcend' himself by noting his own foibles" [all emphases in original] (p. 171). (Comedy, laughing at our own foibles, is not to be confused with humor, laughing at others.) The comic frame can be understood by contrasting it to the tragic frame. The tragic frame sees social ills as the result of human evil. Thus, the correction of social problems requires redemption to purge guilt from the social order. In contrast, comedy accepts human beings as imperfect. Social problems arise not from human evil, but human error and stupidity (Burke, 1984a, p. 41; Carlson, 1986, p. 447–448). Burke wrote mainly about the tragic frame because that perspective, especially in the twentieth century, dominated our view of the world and our view of ourselves, but he felt the comic frame provided "mankind's only hope" to avoid self-destruction (1966, p. 20) and was "the most serviceable for the handling of human relationships" (1984a, p. 106). Burke (1984a) considers comedy the most "humane" (p. 42) and "civilized" (p. 39) form of art. He writes:

> The progress of humane enlightenment can go no further than in picturing people not as *vicious*, but as *mistaken*. When you add that people are *necessarily* mistaken, that all people are exposed to situations in which they must act as fools, that *every* insight contains its own special kind of blindness, you complete the comic circle. [all emphases in original] (Burke, 1984a, p. 41)

Burke's concept of the comic frame may seem similar to the Platonic view that knowledge equals virtue, but it is not. Plato believed that we should seek knowledge because with it we would acquire virtue. In Burke there is more of a recognition that our foibles will always be with us. He asks only that we recognize them. In recognizing our foibles we adopt a wider frame of reference that reduces the tendency to become strict in adherence to one ideology. The comic frame promotes a realistic sense of our own limits (Burke, 1984a, pp. 101–102, 107; Crusius, 1999, p. 207). Burke's point is that instead of labeling our rhetorical opponents as evil, we recognize that they consider themselves just as moral and well intentioned as we consider ourselves to be. We should consider them not evil, but *mistaken*, and recognize that we may also be mistaken in some respects.

In brief, while in the tragic frame actors play the roles of heroes or villains and the plot emphasizes the confrontation with and elimination of evil, in the comic frame everyone is both hero and villain. Although the comic frame allows for change in the social order, it recognizes that some social order must exist for humans to function and that changes in the social order must never be accomplished at the expense of the humanity of those on the other side. Conflict is humanized by the actor's consciousness of his or her own foibles (see Carlson, 1986, p. 448).

Although Burke (1984a) does point out that the literary categories cannot be isolated in purity, that they do overlap somewhat (p. 57), both King and the black power movement can be said to have viewed the civil rights struggle mainly through the frame of tragedy. While King did recognize that good and evil exists in all of us, his rhetoric emphasized the need for good to *triumph over* evil. He saw the civil rights movement largely in moral terms and he saw segregation and racism as not merely mistaken, but as evil and sinful blights upon humankind. Even his largely conciliatory "I Have a Dream" speech characterized his opponents as "vicious racists" and the governor of Alabama as "having his lips dripping with the words of interposition and nullification." The difference, within the perspective of the tragic frame, between King and the black power advocates was that King offered whites redemption for their sins, while black power advocates wanted to leave whites convicted of their guilt and turn their attention to healing the wounds of the black community.

Carlson (1986) contends that King operated in the comic frame because his reliance on Christian spirituality and peaceful goals emphasized identification with all humanity (p. 452). She also contends that "peaceful civil disobedience" illustrates the comic frame because it "overcomes its opponents while still recognizing the value of individual human beings" (pp. 448–449). Carlson is incorrect on both counts. While civil disobedience *per se*, as a tactic, *can* be comic, King certainly did not use it that way. King used civil disobedience to elicit violence and to create a sociodrama of good versus evil in which civil rights demonstrators, and most notably King himself, played the role of tragic heroes and segregationists played the role of villains (see Garrow, 1978, pp. 2–3, 220–231; Fairclough, 1987, pp. 107–109). Birmingham and Selma can hardly be seen as anything but tragedy. And although Christian spirituality did underlie King's rhetoric, he used it not to emphasize the human mistakes and foibles of all people, but to make sharp distinctions between good people and evil people. This had important implications for the civil rights movement. The motives we attribute to ourselves and our opponents dramatically shape our perception of events. Burke (1984a) wrote:

> In the motives we assign to the actions of ourselves and our neighbors, there is implicit a program of socialization. In deciding *why* people do as they do, we get the cues that place us with relation to them. Hence, a vocabulary of motives is important for the forming of both private and public relationships. [emphasis in original] (p. 170)

King's tragic frame saw racists and segregationists as evil and vicious. But a comic frame would have seen them as mistaken, as perpetuators of folly. King's error was to say that because racism is morally evil, those who practice it are morally evil. Violent segregationists committed evil acts, but the vast majority of segregationists were not violent and did not consider themselves evil. They were acting in accordance with the moral values to which they were acculturated. Once the social order declares that those values are "evil," as opposed to being mistaken, one has two choices. One can either withdraw in sullen silence, or appeal to the social order for forgiveness. If the choice is the latter, the priests of the new social order (in this case) are African Americans. Only they can give absolution (a role the black power advocates refused to play). Thus, the rituals of absolution that have developed in our post-civil-rights-era public culture: the Martin Luther King holiday, affirmative action programs, the extreme sensitivity whites often show to saying anything that might get them labeled "racists." If the choice is withdrawal, reconciliation does not take place. For all their legislative successes, King and the civil rights movement were not able to maintain what Hofstadter (1968) refers to as "comity." Comity is the maintenance in public debate of civility. Comity is engaging in public debate without denying the legitimacy of the opponent's values: "The basic humanity of the opposition is not forgotten; civility is not abandoned; the sense that a community life must be carried on after the acerbic issues of the moment have been fought over and won is seldom very far out of mind" (p. 454). Of course, civility broke down on both sides, and segregationists violated this principle long before King ever came along, but it is African Americans who have suffered the more for the failure of the nation to achieve racial reconciliation. It is the winners of the debate who are responsible for maintaining comity. They must win in a way that allows the opposition to rejoin the community without a loss of face. But this did not happen after the civil rights debate. Former segregationists, for the most part, either sought redemption or withdrew from the debate, and the courts implemented the civil rights agenda of busing and affirmative action programs that is still being challenged today because a true national consensus to implement these programs was never achieved.

A civil rights movement from the comic frame would have placed less emphasis on moralistic good versus evil arguments—good blacks and good whites versus bad whites, as King saw it; or blacks (good) versus whites (bad), as many black power advocates saw it—and more emphasis on how segregation and racism is another example of the folly and stupidity we human beings are prone to falling into. This could be done without ignoring the evil effects of the mistaken intellectual notion of racism. When someone is declared mistaken, as opposed to evil, then he or she can be reconciled to the social order without as great a loss of face. A comic approach might have avoided the playing out of the tragic drama of white guilt and black victimage that has been the legacy of the civil rights movement. A comic approach could have allowed us to transcend our differences, not by appealing to vague and illusory socioreligious mythology, but by sharing the knowledge of our own ignorance, stupidity, and shortcomings. A tragic view of the history of American race relations requires reparations of some type (whether economic or moral) for something which can never be made up for—three-hundred-plus years of slavery, segregation, discrimination, and racial oppression—and for which the original perpetuators are all dead. A comic perspective would not ignore or forgive this, but reclassify it. Burke (1984a) writes:

> The comic frame, in making a man the student of himself, makes it possible for him to "transcend" occasions when he has been tricked or cheated, since he can readily put such discouragements in his "assets" column, under the head of "experience." Thus we "win" by subtly changing the rules of the game—and by a mere trick of bookkeeping . . . we make "assets" out of "liabilities." (p. 171)

A comic frame of reference would not have convicted whites of guilt as much as of folly and ignorance, perhaps dissipating white shame and embarrassment and allowing greater racial reconciliation. A comic frame might have prevented the association of black power with black victimage and black moral superiority, acknowledging the humanity of black people through their shared fallibility with all people instead of through their unique experience of suffering and oppression.

NOTE

1. The following treatment of the ideas and philosophy of black power is derived mainly from the following sources: Carmichael (1966); Lester (1966); Barbour (Ed.) (1968); Harding (1968); and Newman (1987), which contains reprints of Newman's essays and lectures on black power from 1966 to 1970.

8

Conclusion

Kenneth Burke's theory of guilt-purification-redemption provides a useful methodology for analyzing Martin Luther King, Jr.'s "I Have a Dream" speech and revealing the persuasive appeals at work in the speech. The guilt-purification-redemption model allows the critic to demonstrate how King's rhetoric elicits and exploits a latent sense of guilt in the minds of his auditors, both black and white, and provides symbolic purification of that guilt through victimage/mortification, transcendence, and images of change, movement, and dramatic catharsis. Through application of Burke's theory of transcendence I have been able to demonstrate how King draws upon powerful images of American secular mythology and then strengthens those images by placing them within the context of divine authority and spiritual redemption. This model also allows an explication of King's elision of social and racial division under transcendent, unitary principles.

Through the use of contemporary metaphor theory, I have been able to demonstrate how King's metaphors function in the speech to reinforce the redemption drama and the elision of social division. King's metaphors simplify complex social/moral issues by predicating those issues in terms of financial obligations and antithetical, binary opposition. His metaphors also ascribe to the audience an essentially passive role in the social drama of the civil rights movement.

Because Martin Luther King and this speech have become cultural icons, this speech has shaped subsequent public discourse and thinking on civil rights, providing a legacy of dealing with America's racial problems in terms of secular and religious mythology and muting other African American voices who attempted to provide an alternative viewpoint on race relations in America. King's assimilationist vision would have been well served to incorporate a critique from the black power perspective that more realistically acknowledged the difficulty of overcoming centuries of racial division and oppression in America. The weakness of the black power perspective, however, and the reason it was largely rejected by mainstream America, was that it provided no transcendent, unity principles under which the nation could unite. King's assimilationist rhetoric incorporated and exploited America's basic myths about itself as a nation with a mission to provide freedom and opportunity for all on an equal basis, but at the expense of eliding the difficulties of achieving such assimilation.

The guilt-purification-redemption form has proven extremely useful in understanding Martin Luther King, Jr.'s "I Have a Dream" speech. Less-developed versions of this theory have been used to examine other examples of discourse (see Brummett, 1981; Elwood, 1989; Mechling and Mechling, 1983; Williamson, 2002), but this book points to a need for rhetorical scholars to identify and analyze other situations in which the redemption of guilt might prove to be an important motivational structure. This book helps rhetorical scholars better understand King's rhetoric, but more study of King's rhetoric, taking into account these findings, needs to be done. Orr's (1990) analysis of King's "Eulogy for the Martyred Children" found that the speech portrays the girls killed in the bombing of the Sixteenth Street Baptist Church as martyrs whose death was an act of victimage with the power to redeem the South. Other speeches by King should also be examined to see if they contain images of purification and redemption. Also, considering that King's rhetoric in his later years contained harsher criticisms of American society, studies could consider how King's rhetoric evolved over the course of his public career (Bobbitt and Mixon, 1994, have made a modest attempt at this). Did he employ the redemptive form less often as he became more radical in his later years, and if so what form, if any, marked his later rhetoric?

The primary direction in which we can take this theory is in extensions and applications of the theory of guilt-purification-redemption, considering the concept of guilt, modes of purification, and the continuing effectiveness of the guilt-purification-redemption form in light of changes in American culture since the time of King's speech.

Burke's concept of guilt is useful for identifying motive structures that may initiate the need for redress or reconciliation to which rhetors may respond. More theoretical studies into the concept of guilt itself, and the sources of guilt, are warranted. For example, what do the things people in a particular culture feel guilty about tell us about that culture? What is the relationship between particular sources of guilt and the modes of purification used to absolve that guilt?

Much more work needs to be done into the modes of purification. We need to better understand the Burkean modes we are familiar with, as well as to identify other modes in which purification may be effected. We need to better understand what new forms purification may take as societies change, and the implications for the audience, and society in general, when any particular mode is employed. For example, might some modes be "better" (i.e., more humane, more effective) than others? Which forms work best in which situations? What would a study of the mode or modes dominant in a particular culture reveal about that culture?

Further study into particular modes developed in this study from Burke's categories is also warranted. For example, we need further research into the rhetorical effect of being a victim, that is, study of the impact of portrayals of the victimization and suffering of one's racial, ethnic, or sexual group. These types of studies have largely been ignored by rhetorical critics because of the fear of implying offense to victimized groups. But to study the rhetorical effect of portrayals and symbolizations of the suffering and victimization of a group is not to deny the actuality or validity of that experience.

In addition, there are other modes of purification that need further study. What other ways may transcendence be effected? Is transcendence a more humane and unifying form of purification than the others? Does transcendence necessarily elide the practical difficulties of achieving unification, as this book argues? Also, there is a need for other studies to demonstrate the multiplicity of ways in which symbolizations of change, movement, and transformations of various types (physical, social, psychological, and spiritual), and dramatic catharsis could serve purificatory functions.

Further research into other (non-Burkean) modes of purification is warranted. For example, despite the fact that hard work seems to be a common form of purification, especially in American culture, it is only briefly mentioned in the literature (Carroll, 1985, p. 39; Solomon, 1980, p. 61). This form could be applicable, for instance, to participants in social movements and political campaigns. No study of which I am aware has demonstrated how the act of working in a cause, movement, or political campaign, in and of itself, can have purificatory effects for the participants. Participation itself, the work and the sense of being involved, can be redemptive. Perhaps this could be studied as a type of transcendence in which the individual is transcending the self for a larger purpose, for a sense of involvement in a larger cause. Other actions, and symbolizations of actions, such as humor, the paying of reparations, washing, singing, and praying (see chapter 6) could be studied as modes of purification.

If the redemption drama is America's metanarrative, as some have argued (see Duncan, 1962, p. 320; Jewett and Lawrence, 1988, p. xxi; Robertson, 1980, pp. 25–26) then what have been the consequences of that for the shaping of public discourse? (See chapter 6 where I suggest some lines of inquiry in answer to that question.) Also, is the redemption drama still as potent a form as it once was in American culture or has it decreased in effectiveness? Has or will American society become self-reflexive about a particular form of purification (i.e., recognizing it as a ritual of purification), and does that decrease its effectiveness? Has or will the American society become self-reflexive about the redemption drama itself, thus causing it to cease to have valence? And finally, have changes in American society since the 1960s—such as a decrease in adherence to traditional Christian convictions, a decrease in belief in America's founding secular myths in the wake of Vietnam, Watergate, and the social upheavals of the 1960s, and the increasing fragmentation of American society into competing ethnic and interest groups—rendered the redemption drama less potent as a rhetorical form for shaping a discourse of national purpose and meaning?

Because of the role Martin Luther King, Jr., has assumed in America as a national hero, and because of reluctance to seem critical of what Martin Luther King stood for, rhetorical critics have been somewhat averse to analyzing King's rhetoric in a way which would imply that it contained any shortcomings. There has been a disinclination to apply the tools of rhetorical criticism to King in a manner as stringent as would be applied to most other rhetors. Most analyses of King's rhetoric seek mainly to praise King's oratorical ability, identify the sources of his ideas, or explain the reasons for his rhetorical effectiveness. Some studies of King's rhetoric even border on the hagiographic (see, for example, Osborn, 1989).

It has not been my purpose to find fault with King's rhetoric in the "Dream" speech merely to be a contrarian, but to show him the respect any great orator deserves by providing a serious critical analysis of his rhetoric and its impact. By better comprehending the persuasive appeals underlying King's discourse, which have so shaped our thinking about the civil rights movement, we can come to a better understanding of where we are today in regard to race relations and how we got here. My research into this subject has not only helped me answer the questions I set out to answer, but also affected my personal intellectual development. I have come to have a great appreciation for Martin Luther King and his ideas. However, there has been a tendency in American culture to idealize and idolize Martin Luther King. In my opinion, this is a mistake. King should not be seen as an idealized hero. He should be seen as a human being who was great not because he was perfect, but because despite his human imperfections he accomplished many great things. We owe him, and ourselves, an honest assessment of those accomplishments. I will give the last word to Charles Willie, one of King's Morehouse College classmates, as quoted by David Garrow:

> By idolizing those whom we honor, we do a disservice to them and to ourselves. By exalting the accomplishments of Martin Luther King, Jr., into a legendary tale that is annually told, we fail to recognize his humanity—his personal and public struggles—that are similar to yours and mine. By idolizing those whom we honor, we fail to realize that we could go and do likewise. (Garrow, 1986a, p. 625)

References

All's set for march of 100,000 on D.C. (1963, August 28). *The Washington Post*, pp. 1, A7.

Alvarez, A. (1988). Martin Luther King's "I Have a Dream": The speech event as metaphor. *Journal of Black Studies*, *18*, 337–357.

American Rhetoric. (2002). *Top 100 American speeches of the 20th century*. Retrieved August 15, 2002, from http://americanrhetoric.com/newtop100speeches.htm

Ansbro, J. J. (1982). *Martin Luther King, Jr.: The making of a mind*. New York: Orbis.

Aristotle. (1954). *The rhetoric and the poetics of Aristotle* (W. R. Roberts and I. Bywater, Trans.). New York: Random House.

Baldwin, L. V. (1984–1985). Martin Luther King, Jr., the black church, and the black messianic vision. *Journal of the Interdenominational Theological Center*, *12*, 93–108.

Baldwin, L. V. (1991). *There is a balm in Gilead: The cultural roots of Martin Luther King, Jr.* Minneapolis: Fortress Press.

Barbour, F. B. (Ed.). (1968). *The black power revolt: A collection of essays*. Boston: Porter Sargent.

Beardsley, M. C. (1962). The metaphorical twist. *Philosophy and Phenomenological Research*, *22*, 293–307.

Berthold, C. A. (1976). Kenneth Burke's cluster-agon method: Its development and an application. *Central States Speech Journal*, *27*, 302–309.

Biggest protest march. (1963, November). *Ebony*, pp. 29–31.

The big man is Martin Luther King, Jr. (1963, July 29). *Newsweek*, pp. 30–31.

Black, E. (1970). The second persona. *Quarterly Journal of Speech*, *56*, 109–119.

Black, M. (1962). *Models and metaphors*. Ithaca, NY: Cornell University Press.

Black power: A statement by the National Committee of Negro Churchmen, July 31, 1966 (1968). In F. B. Barbour (Ed.), *The black power revolt: A collection of essays* (pp. 264–272). Boston: Porter Sargent.

Bobbitt, D. A., and Mixon, H. (1994). Prophecy and apocalypse in the rhetoric of Martin Luther King, Jr. *The Journal of Communication and Religion*, *17* (1), 27–38.

Booth, W. C. (1978). Metaphor as rhetoric: The problem of evaluation. *Critical Inquiry*, *5*, 49–72.

Boulware, M. H. (1969). *The oratory of Negro leaders: 1900–1968*. Westport, CT: Negro Universities Press.

Branch, T. (1988). *Parting the waters: America in the King years, 1954–63*. New York: Simon and Schuster.

Brock, B. L. (1980). Rhetorical criticism: A Burkeian approach. In B. L. Brock and R. L. Scott (Eds.), *Methods of rhetorical criticism* (pp. 348–360). Detroit: Wayne State University Press.

Brummett, B. (1981). Burkean scapegoating, mortification, and transcendence in presidential campaign rhetoric. *Central States Speech Journal*, *32*, 254–264.

Brummett, B. (1982). Burkean transcendence and ultimate terms in rhetoric by and about James Watt. *Central States Speech Journal*, *33*, 547–556.

Brummett, B. (1984a). Burke's representative anecdote as a method in media criticism. *Critical Studies in Mass Communication*, *1*, 161–176.

Brummett, B. (1984b). The representative anecdote as a Burkean method, applied to evangelical rhetoric. *Southern Speech Communication Journal*, *50*, 1–23.

Buber, M. (1965). Guilt and guilt feelings. In *The knowledge of man* (pp. 121–148) (M. Friedman, Trans.). New York: Harper & Row.

Burke, K. (1947). Ideology and myth. *Accent*, 7, 195–205.

Burke, K. (1966). *Language as symbolic action*. Berkeley: University of California Press.

Burke, K. (1968a). *Counter-statement*. Berkeley: University of California Press. (Original work published 1931)

Burke, K. (1968b). Dramatism. In D. L. Sills (Ed.), *International encyclopedia of the social sciences* (Vol. 7) (pp. 445–452). New York: Macmillan and Free Press.

Burke, K. (1969a). *A grammar of motives*. Berkeley: University of California Press. (Original work published 1945)

Burke, K. (1969b). *A rhetoric of motives*. Berkeley: University of California Press. (Original work published 1950)

Burke, K. (1970). *The rhetoric of religion*. Berkeley: University of California Press. (Original work published 1961)

Burke, K. (1973). *The philosophy of literary form* (3rd ed.). Berkeley: University of California Press. (Original work published 1941)

Burke, K. (1984a). *Attitudes toward history* (3rd ed.). Berkeley: University of California Press. (Original work published 1937)

Burke, K. (1984b). *Permanence and change* (3rd ed.). Berkeley: University of California Press. (Original work published 1935)

Carlson, A. C. (1986). Gandhi and the comic frame: "Ad bellum purificandum." *Quarterly Journal of Speech*, *72*, 446–455.

Carlson, A. C. (Ed.). (1988). Limitations on the comic frame: Some witty American women of the nineteenth century. *Quarterly Journal of Speech*, *74*, 310–322.

Carmichael, S. (1966). Toward black liberation. *The Massachusetts Reveiw*, *7*, 639–651.

Carpenter, R. H. (1990). America's tragic metaphor: Our twentieth-century combatants as frontiersmen. *Quarterly Journal of Speech, 76*, 1–22.

Carson, C. (Ed.) (1997). *The Papers of Martin Luther King, Jr.* (Vol. 3). Berkeley: University of California Press.

Carroll, J. (1985). *Guilt: The grey eminence behind character, history and culture.* London: Routledge & Kegan Paul.

Cartwright, J. H. (1989). The social eschatology of Martin Luther King, Jr. In D. G. Garrow (Ed.), *Martin Luther King, Jr.: Civil rights leader, theologian, orator* (Vol. 1) (pp. 161–170). Brooklyn, NY: Carlson.

Chafe, W. H. (1986). The end of one struggle, the beginning of another. In C. W. Eagles (Ed.), *The civil rights movement in America* (pp. 127–148). Jackson: University Press of Mississippi.

Childs, M. W. (1963, August 29). Demonstration proves answer to scoffers hoping for worst. *St. Louis Post–Dispatch*, pp. 1D, 20D.

Clark, K. B. (1963). *The Negro protest.* Boston: Beacon.

Colaiaco, J. A. (1988). *Martin Luther King, Jr.: Apostle of militant nonviolence.* New York: St. Martin's Press.

Colston, F. C. (1979). The ideology of black power: An assessment. *Western Journal of Black Studies, 3*, 233–243.

Condit, C. M. (1991, November). Post-Burke: Transcending the substance of dramatism. Paper presented at the annual convention of the Speech Communication Association, Atlanta, GA.

Cone, J. H. (1984). Martin Luther King, Jr., black theology–black church. *Theology Today, 41*, 409–420.

Cone, J. H. (1986). The theology of Martin Luther King, Jr. *Union Seminary Quarterly Review, 40*, 21–39.

Congressional record–Senate. (1963, September 3). Vol. 109, 88th Congress, First Session.

Conrad, C. (1981). Agon and rhetorical form: The essence of "old feminist" rhetoric. *Central States Speech Journal, 32*, 45–53.

Conrad, C. (1984). Phases, pentads, and dramatistic critical process. *Central State Speech Journal, 35*, 94–104.

Cox, J. R. (1989). The fulfillment of time: King's "I Have a Dream" speech (August 28, 1963). In M. C. Leff and F. J. Kauffeld (Eds.), *Texts in context* (pp. 181–204). Davis, CA: Hermagoras.

Crable, B. (2000). Burke's perspective on perspectives: Grounding dramatism in the representative anecdote. *Quarterly Journal of Speech, 86*, 318–333.

Crusius, T. W. (1999). *Kenneth Burke and the conversation after philosophy.* Carbondale: Southern Illinois University Press.

Dallek, R. (2003). *An unfinished life: John F. Kennedy, 1917–1963.* Boston: Little, Brown.

Derrida, J. (1982). *Margins of philosophy* (A. Bass, Trans.). Chicago: University of Chicago Press.

Downing, F. L. (1986). *To see the promised land: The faith pilgrimage of Martin Luther King*, Jr. Macon, GA: Mercer University Press.

Duncan, H. D. (1962). *Communication and social order*. New York: Bedminster.

Duncan, H. D. (1968). *Symbols in society*. New York: Oxford University Press.

Dyson, M. E. (2000). *I may not get there with you: The true Martin Luther King, Jr.* New York: The Free Press.

Edsall, T. B., and Edsall, M. D. (1991). *Chain reaction: The impact of race, rights, and taxes on American politics*. New York: W. W. Norton.

Elwood, W. N. (1989). Call for Philip Morris: Redeeming smokers through the drama of protest rhetoric. *Florida Communication Journal*, *17*, 23–28.

Excerpts from remarks made at civil rights program. (1963, August 29). *The Washington Post,* p. A14.

Fairclough, A. (1987). *To redeem the soul of America: The Southern Christian Leadership Conference and Martin Luther King, Jr.* Athens: University of Georgia Press.

Forman, J. (1972). *The making of black revolutionaries*. New York: Macmillan.

Foss, S. K., Foss, K. A., and Trapp, R. (1985). *Contemporary perspectives on rhetoric*. Prospect Heights, IL: Waveland.

Foucault, M. (1972). *The archeology of knowledge* (A. M. S. Smith, Trans.). New York: Pantheon.

Frazer, J. G. (1911–1915). *The golden bough: A study in magic and religion* (3rd ed., 12 vols.). London: Macmillan.

Fullinwider, S. P. (1969). *The mind and mood of black America*. Homewood, IL: Dorsey.

Garber, P. R. (1974–1975). King was a black theologian. *Journal of Religious Thought*, *31*, 16–32.

Garrow, D. J. (1978). *Protest at Selma: Martin Luther King, Jr., and the Voting Rights Act of 1965*. New Haven and London: Yale University Press.

Garrow, D. J. (1986a). *Bearing the cross: Martin Luther King, Jr., and the Southern Christian Leadership Conference*. New York: William Morrow.

Garrow, D. J. (1986b). The intellectual development of Martin Luther King, Jr.: Influences and commentaries. *Union Seminary Quarterly Review*, *40*, 5–20.

Gentile, T. (1983). *March on Washington: August 28, 1963*. Washington, D.C.: New Day Publications.

Goldzwig, S. R., and Dionisopoulos, G. N. (1989). John F. Kennedy's civil rights discourse: The evolution from "principled bystander" to public advocate. *Communication Monographs*, *56*, 179–198.

Graham, H. D. (1990). *The civil rights era: Origins and development of national policy, 1960–1972*. New York: Oxford University Press.

Grassi, E. (1980). *Rhetoric as philosophy: The humanist tradition* (J. M. Krois and A. Azodi, Trans.). University Park: Pennsylvania State University Press.

Gravlee, G. J. (1987). A black rhetoric of social revolution. In C. M. Logue and H. Dorgan (Eds.), *A new diversity in contemporary southern rhetoric* (pp. 52–88). Baton Rouge: Louisiana State University Press.

Griffin, L. M. (1969). A dramatistic theory of the rhetoric of movements. In W. H. Rueckert (Ed.), *Critical responses to Kenneth Burke*. Minneapolis: University of Minnesota Press.

Hampton, H., and Fayer, S. (Eds.). (1990). Voices of freedom: An oral history of the civil rights movement from the 1950s through the 1980s. New York: Bantam.

Hanigan, J. P. (1974). Martin Luther King, Jr.: The images of a man. *Journal of Religious Thought, 31* , 68–95.

Hansen, D. D. (2003). *The dream: Martin Luther King, Jr. and the speech that inspired a nation*. New York: HarperCollins.

Hare, N. (1965). *The black anglo-saxons*. New York: Marzani & Munsell.

Harding, V. (1968). The religion of black power. In D. E. Cutler (Ed.), *The religious situation: 1968* (pp. 3–38). Boston: Beacon Press.

Hariman, R. (1989). Time and the reconstitution of gradualism in King's address: A response to Cox. In M. C. Leff and F. J. Kauffeld (Eds.), *Texts in context* (pp. 205–217). Davis, CA: Hermagoras.

Havelock, E. A. (1963). *Preface to Plato*. Cambridge, MA: Harvard University Press.

Heath, R. L. (1989). Kenneth Burke's poetics and the influence of I. A. Richards: A cornerstone for dramatism. *Communication Studies*, *40*, 54–65.

Heffner, R. D. (Ed.). (1985). *A documentary history of the United States* (4th ed.). New York: New American Library.

Heidegger, M. (1962). *Being and time* (J. Macquarrie and E. Robinson, Trans.). San Francisco: Harper & Row.

Henry, C. P. (1987). Delivering Daniel: The dialectic of ideology and theology in the thought of Martin Luther King, Jr. *Journal of Black Studies*, *17*, 327–345.

Hernton, C. C. (1966). *White papers for white Americans*. Garden City, NY: Doubleday.

Hoban, J. L., Jr. (1980). Rhetorical rituals of rebirth. *Quarterly Journal of Speech*, *66*, 275–288.

Hofstadter, R. (1968). *The progressive historians*. Chicago: University of Chicago Press.

Ivie, R. (1980). Images of savagery in American justifications for war. *Communication Monographs*, *47*, 279–294.

Ivie, R. (1982). The metaphor of force in prowar discourse: The case of 1812. *Quarterly Journal of Speech*, *68*, 240–253.

Ivie, R. (1987). Metaphor and the rhetorical invention of cold war "idealists." *Communication Monographs*, *54*, 165–182.

Ivie, R. (1988, April). Kenneth Burke on metaphor and motive. Paper presented at the annual convention of the Southern States Communication Association, Memphis, TN.

Jamieson, K. H. (1980). The metaphoric cluster in the rhetoric of Pope Paul VI and Edmund G. Brown, Jr. *Quarterly Journal of Speech*, *66*, 51–72.

Jewett, R. (1973). *The Captain America complex: The dilemma of zealous nationalism*. Philadelphia: Westminster Press.

Jewett, R., and Lawrence, J. S. (1988). *The American monomyth* (2nd ed.). Lanham, MD: University Press of America.

Johnson, M. (1981). Introduction: Metaphor in the philosophical tradition. In M. Johnson (Ed.), *Philosophical perspectives on metaphor* (pp. 3–47). Minneapolis: University of Minnesota Press.

Jung, C. (1960). The transcendent function. In *The structure and dynamics of the psyche* (pp. 67–91), Vol. 8 of *The collected works of C. G. Jung* (20 vols.) (R. F. C. Hull, et al., Trans.). New York: Pantheon.

Kendall, W. (1965). The civil rights movement and the coming constitutional crisis. *The Intercollegiate Review*, *1*(2), 53–66.

King, A. A. (1971). The rhetorical legacy of the black church. *Central States Speech Journal*, *22*, 179–185.

King, C. S. (1969). *My life with Martin Luther King, Jr.* New York: Holt, Rinehart and Winston.

King, M. L., Jr. (1957a). Facing the challenge of a new age. *The Phylon Quarterly*, *18*, 24–34.

King, M. L., Jr. (1957b, September 2). The look to the future. Box 6, Folder 29, Mississippi Valley Collection, University of Memphis Libraries, Memphis, TN.

King, M. L., Jr. (1958). *Stride toward freedom: The Montgomery story*. New York: Harper & Row.

King, M. L., Jr. (1963a). Address at march in Detroit—June 23, 1963. King Library and Archives, The Martin Luther King, Jr. Center for Nonviolent Social Change, Atlanta, GA.

King, M. L., Jr. (1963b). Advance text of speech to be delivered by Dr. Martin Luther King, Jr., March on Washington, August 28, 1963. King Library and Archives, The Martin Luther King, Jr. Center for Nonviolent Social Change, Atlanta, GA.

King, M. L., Jr. (1963c, August 28). I have a dream. On *Great speeches* [videotape] (Vol. 1). R. Cook (executive producer). Alliance Video, 1985.

King, M. L., Jr. (1963d, August 28). I have a dream. In R. F. Reid (Ed.) *Three centuries of American rhetorical discourse* (pp. 723–726). Prospect Heights, IL: Waveland, 1988.

King, M. L., Jr. (1964a). Statement to the press regarding the Nobel trip, December 4, 1964. King Library and Archives, The Martin Luther King, Jr. Center for Nonviolent Social Change, Atlanta, GA.

King, M. L., Jr. (1964b). The sword that heals. *The Critic*, *22* (6), 6–14.

King, M. L., Jr. (1981). *Strength to love*. Philadelphia: Fortress Press. (Original work published 1963)

King, M. L., Jr. (1986). *A testament of hope: The essential writings of Martin Luther King, Jr.*, J. M. Washington (Ed.). New York: Harper & Row.

Koestler, A. (1978). *Janus: A summing up*. New York: Random House.

Leff, M. C. (1983). Topical invention and metaphoric interaction. *Southern Speech Communication Journal*, *48*, 214–229.

Leff, M. C. (1987, November). Metaphoric action in King's "I Have a Dream" speech. Paper presented at the annual meeting of the Speech Communication Association, Boston, MA.

Lentz, R. (1990). *Symbols, the news magazines, and Martin Luther King, Jr.* Baton Rouge: Louisiana State University Press.

Lester, J. (1966). The angry children of Malcolm X. *Sing Out! 16* (5), 20–25.

Lewis, D. L. (1978). *King: A biography* (2nd ed.). Urbana: University of Illinois Press.

Lindsay, S. A. (1998). *Implicit rhetoric: Kenneth Burke's extension of Aristotle's concept of entelechy*. Lanham, MD: University Press of America.

Lischer, R. (1995). *The preacher King: Martin Luther King, Jr. and the word that moved America*. New York: Oxford University Press.

Loury, G. (1989). Black political culture after the sixties. In P. Collier and D. Horowitz (Eds.), *Former radicals look back at the sixties* (pp. 141–148). Lanham, MD: Madison.

Lucaites, J. L., and Condit, C. M. (1990). Reconstructing "equality": Culturetypal and counter-cultural rhetoric in the martyred black vision. *Communication Monographs*, *57*, 5–24.

Madsen, A. (1993). Burke's representative anecdote as a critical method. In J. W. Chesebro (Ed.), *Extensions of the Burkeian system* (pp. 208–229). Tuscaloosa: University of Alabama Press.

Malcolm X. (1965). *Malcolm X speaks*. G. Breitman (Ed.). New York: Grove Weidenfeld.

Marable, M. (1984). *Race, reform and rebellion: The second reconstruction in black America*, 1945–1982. Jackson: University Press of Mississippi.

Marable, M. (1985). *Black American politics: From the Washington marches to Jesse Jackson*. London: Verso.

Marbury, C. H. (1989). An excursus on the biblical and theological rhetoric of Martin Luther King. In D. G. Garrow (Ed.), *Martin Luther King, Jr.: Civil rights leader, theologian, orator* (Vol. 3) (pp. 623–634). Brooklyn, NY: Carlson.

The march in Washington. (1963, August 30). *Time*, p. 11.

The march of time. (1973, September 10). *Newsweek*, pp. 24–26.

Mechling, E. M., and Mechling, J. (1983). Sweet talk: The moral rhetoric against sugar. *Central States Speech Journal*, *34*, 19–32.

Meier, A. (1965). On the role of Martin Luther King. *New Politics*, *4*, 52–59.

Merk, F. (1963). *Manifest destiny and mission in American history*. New York: Vintage.

Metz, J. B. (1977). Redemption and emancipation. *Cross Currents*, *27*, 321–336.

Miller, K. D. (1988). Epistemology of a drum major: Martin Luther King, Jr. and the black folk pulpit. *Rhetoric Society Quarterly*, *18*, 225–236.

Miller, K. D. (1989). Voice merging and self-making: The epistemology of "I Have a Dream." *Rhetoric Society Quarterly*, *19*, 23–31.

Miller, K. D. (1992). *Voice of deliverance: The language of Martin Luther King, Jr. and its sources*. New York: The Free Press.

Miller, K. D. (1993). Alabama as Egypt: Martin Luther King, Jr., and the religion of slaves. In C. Calloway-Thomas and J. L. Luciates (Eds.), *Martin Luther King, Jr., and the sermonic power of public discourse*. Tuscaloosa: University of Alabama Press.

Morone, J.A. (2003). *Hellfire nation: The politics of sin in American history*. New Haven and London: Yale University Press.

Newman, R. (1987). *Black power and black religion: Essays and reviews*. West Cornwall, CT: Locust Hill Press.

Nieli, R. (1991). Ethnic tribalism and human personhood. In R. Nieli (Ed.), *Racial preference and racial justice: The new affirmative action controversy* (pp. 61–103). Washington, DC: Ethics and Public Policy Center.

Nietzsche, F. (2001). On truth and lies in a nonmoral sense (D. Breazeale, Ed. and Trans.). In P. Bizzell and B. Herzberg (Eds.), *The rhetorical tradition: Readings from classical times to the present* (2nd ed.) (pp. 1171–1179). Boston: Bedford/St. Martin's.

Nisbet, R. (1975). *Twilight of authority*. New York: Oxford University Press.

Oates, S. B. (1982). *Let the trumpet sound: The life of Martin Luther King, Jr.* New York: Harper & Row.

O'Brien, M. (1988). Old myths/new insights: History and Dr. King. *The History Teacher*, *22*, 48–65.

Orr, C. M. (1990, November). Martin Luther King, Jr.'s "Eulogy for the Martyred children": A drama of victimage and redemption. Paper presented at the annual meeting of the Speech Communication Association, Chicago, IL.

Osborn, M. (1967a). Archetypal metaphor in rhetoric: The light–dark family. *Quarterly Journal of Speech*, *53*, 115–126.

Osborn, M. M. (1967b). The evolution of the theory of metaphor in rhetoric. *Western Speech*, *31*, 121–131.

Osborn, M. (1977). The evolution of the archetypal sea in rhetoric and poetic. *Quarterly Journal of Speech*, *63*, 347–363.

Osborn, M. (1989). "I've Been to the Mountaintop": The critic as participant. In M. C. Leff and F. J. Kauffeld (Eds.), *Texts in context* (pp. 149–166). Davis, CA: Hermagoras.

Osborn, M. (1990, April). Martin Luther King, Jr. and the concept of great speaking. Paper presented at the annual meeting of the Southern States Communication Association, Birmingham, AL.

Osborn, M. M., and Ehninger, D. (1962). The metaphor in public address. *Speech Monographs*, *29*, 223–234.

The Oxford English dictionary. (1989). (20 vols.). Prepared by J. A. Simpson and E. S. C. Weiner. Oxford: Oxford University Press.

Parman, S. (1991). *Dream and culture: An anthropological study of the western intellectual tradition*. New York: Praeger.

Patterson, E. (1963, August 29). In the shadow of Abe Lincoln, a voice shouts for freedom. *The Atlanta Constitution*, pp. 1, 14.

Patton, J. H. (1993). " I Have a Dream": The performance of theology fused with the power of orality. In C. Calloway-Thomas and J. L. Luciates (Eds.), *Martin Luther King, Jr. and the sermonic power of public discourse* (pp. 104–126). Tuscaloosa: University of Alabama Press.

Payne, D. (1989). *Coping with failure: The therapeutic uses of rhetoric*. Columbia: University of South Carolina Press.

Perera, S. B. (1986). *The scapegoat complex: Toward a mythology of shadow and guilt*. Toronto, Canada: Inner City Books.

Pfeffer, P. F. (1990). *A. Philip Randolph, pioneer of the civil rights movement*. Baton Rouge: Louisiana State University Press.

Prime numbers (2003, June 20). *The Chronicle of Higher Education*, p. A7.

Poussaint, A. F. (1968). The Negro American: His self-image and integration. In F. B. Barbour (Ed.), *The black power revolt: A collection of essays* (pp. 94–102). Boston: Porter Sargent.

Rauschenbusch, W. (1907). *Christianity and the social crisis*. New York: Macmillan.

Rauschenbusch, W. (1960). *A theology for the social gospel*. New York and Nashville: Abingdon. (Original work published 1917)

Reik, T. (1957). *Myth and guilt*. New York: George Braziller.

Reston, J. (1963, August 29). "I have a dream. . . ." *The New York Times*, pp. 1, 17.

Richards, I. A. (1936). *The philosophy of rhetoric*. London: Oxford University Press.

Ricoeur, P. (1973). Creativity in language. *Philosophy Today*, *17*, 97–111.

Ricoeur, P. (1977). *The rule of metaphor* (R. Czerny, Trans.). Toronto: University of Toronto Press.

Ricoeur, P. (1978). The metaphorical process as cognition, imagination and feeling. *Critical Inquiry*, *5*, 143–159.

Robertson, J. O. (1980). *American myth, American reality*. New York: Hill and Wang.

Rorabaugh, W. J. (2002). *Kennedy and the promise of the sixties*. Cambridge, U.K.: Cambridge University Press.

Rueckert, W. H. (1982). *Kenneth Burke and the drama of human relations* (2nd ed.). Berkeley: University of California Press.

Russell, B. (1950). The superior virtue of the oppressed. In *Unpopular essays* (pp. 58–64). New York: Simon and Schuster.

Scheibel, D. (2002). The cat with the "strat" comes back: A Burkeian–Weickian primer for organizing nature. *Southern Communication Journal, 67*, 303–318.

Scott, R. L. (1968). Black power bends Martin Luther King. *Speaker and Gavel*, *5*, 80–86.

Singh, L. P., and Sirisena, B. M. (1988). *Zen Buddhism*. New York: Envoy Press.

Sleeper, J. (1990). *The closest of strangers: Liberalism and the politics of race in New York*. New York: W. W. Norton.

Smith, D. H. (1964). Martin Luther King, Jr.: Rhetorician of revolt. *Dissertation Abstracts International*, 25, 2749-A (University Microfilms No. 64-12753).

Smith, D. H. (1970). An exegesis of Martin Luther King, Jr.'s social philosophy. *Phylon*, *31*, 89–97.

Smith, K. L., and Zepp, I. G. (1974). *Search for the beloved community: The thinking of Martin Luther King, Jr*. Valley Forge, PA: Judson.

Solomon, M. (1980). Redemptive rhetoric: The continuity motif in the rhetoric of Right to Life. *Central States Speech Journal*, *31*, 52–62.

Solomon, M. (1993). Covenanted rights: The metaphoric matrix of "I Have a Dream." In C. Calloway-Thomas and J. L. Luciates (Eds.), *Martin Luther King, Jr. and the sermonic power of public discourse* (pp. 66–84). Tuscaloosa: University of Alabama Press.

Spillers, H. J. (1971). Martin Luther King and the style of the black sermon. *Black Scholar*, *3,* 14–27.

Steele, S. (1990). *The content of our character: A new vision of race in America*. New York: St. Martin's Press.

Taylor, C. (1985). Interpretation and the sciences of man. In *Philosophy and the human sciences: Philosophical papers* (Vol. 2) (pp. 15–57). Cambridge: Cambridge University Press.

Terrell, R. (1989). Discarding the dream. In D. J. Garrow (Ed.), *Martin Luther King, Jr.: Civil rights leader, theologian, orator* (Vol. 3) (pp. 971–995). Brooklyn, NY: Carlson.

This is SCLC. (no date). [pamphlet, circa late 1950s]. King Library and Archives, The Martin Luther King, Jr. Center for Nonviolent Social Change, Atlanta, GA.

Thorton, J. M., III (1986). Commentary [On Chafe (1986)]. In C. W. Eagles (Ed.), *The civil rights movement in America* (pp. 148–155). Jackson: University Press of Mississippi.

Threats: Negroes' latest weapon in rights drive. (1963, July 1). *U.S. News & World Report*, pp. 39–40.

Tracy, D. (1975). *Blessed rage for order: The new pluralism in theology*. New York: Seabury Press.

Vivian, C. T. (1970). *Black power and the American myth*. Philadelphia: Fortress Press.

Walton, H., Jr. (1971). *The political philosophy of Martin Luther King, Jr.* Westport, CT: Greenwood.

Warren, M. A. (2001). *King came preaching: The pulpit power of Dr. Martin Luther King, Jr*. Downers Grove, IL: InterVarsity Press.

Washington on stage. (1963, August 28). *The Washinton Post*. p. A16.

Weiss, N. J. (1986). Creative tensions in the leadership of the civil rights movement. In C. W. Eagles (Ed.), *The civil rights movement in America* (pp. 39–55). Jackson: University Press of Mississippi.

Wenzel, J. W. (1989). "A dangerous unselfishness." Martin Luther King, Jr.'s speech at Memphis, April 3, 1968. In M. C. Leff and F. J. Kauffeld (Eds.), *Texts in Context* (pp. 167–179). Davis, CA: Hermugoras.

White, H. (1978). *Tropics of discourse: Essays in cultural criticism*. Baltimore: The Johns Hopkins University Press.

Whitson, S. (1989). "Sanitized for your protection:" On the hygience of metaphors. *Rhetoric Society Quarterly*, *19*, 253–262.

Williamson, L. A. (2002). Racism, tolerance, and perfected redemption: A rhetorical critique of the dragging trial. *Southern Communication Journal*, *67*, 245–258.

Worried leaders. (1963, July 15). *Newsweek*, pp. 19–20.

Wright, N., Jr. (1968). The crisis which bred black power. In F. B. Barbour (Ed.), *The black power revolt: A collection of essays* (pp. 103–118). Boston: Porter Sargent.

Zepp, I. G., Jr. (1989). *The social vision of Martin Luther King, Jr*. Brooklyn, NY: Carlson.

Index

About the Author

David A. Bobbitt is associate professor of communication at Wesleyan College in Macon, Georgia. He has a B.S. from the University of Tennessee, an M.A. from Memphis State University, an M.A. from the University of Iowa, and a Ph.D. from Louisiana State University. Dr. Bobbitt has published articles in the *Journal of Communication and Religion* and the *Florida Communication Journal*.

www.ingramcontent.com/pod-product-compliance
Lightning Source LLC
Chambersburg PA
CBHW071527100726
47908CB00004B/1316

* 9 7 8 0 7 4 2 5 2 9 2 8 1 *